The Word Became Flesh

A Study of the Gospel of John

PAMELA PALAGYI

Arise
PUBLISHING

The Word Became Flesh: A Study of the Gospel of John

Copyright © 2003 by Pamela Palagyi

ISBN 978-1-945084-00-3

4th Printing

Printed in the United States of America 2016

Introduction

Welcome to the world of ancient Israel!

In this in-depth study of the Gospel of John, I invite you to enter into the culture and history of New Testament times. Experience the Messiah with fresh eyes and apply those spiritual principles to your own life.

The Word Became Flesh is an eight-week Bible study on the Gospel of John. The study features:

- *A comprehensive look at the life of Christ seen through John's eyes*

- *Revelation of Jesus through the seven 'I AM" statements and seven signs of the Messiah*

- *Enriching historical and cultural background that makes the Bible come alive*

- *Word studies and commentary that increase understanding of the original text*

- *Personal applications for spiritual growth*

The Bible study is organized to encourage Christ-like development through scripture reading, interpretation, and application of spiritual principles. Each lesson is formatted into sections to promote regular study in the word of God. I have used an inductive approach to encourage each participant to personally interpret the message of the gospel. The readers will find historical and cultural background, word studies, Greek grammar, and Biblical commentary throughout the book. At the close of every chapter, there is opportunity to apply the scriptural principles in a practical way. It is a well-rounded text designed to produce healthy spiritual growth.

The study was first written as a year-long Bible study with twenty-four lessons. I have edited the original version and condensed the twenty-four lessons into eight chapters. This new format will help those groups who are looking for a shorter time frame. For others who want a longer series, I suggest splitting several of the chapters into two-week sessions.

I want to express my gratitude to my husband Paul and my family who continue to patiently support me through the writing process. My heart-felt thanks go especially to my two daughters, Lisa and Laurie, who first edited, formatted, and designed the cover for the study. How wonderful to reap the fruits of their training! Their expertise was invaluable.

I also want to thank my prayer partner and dear friend Pat Satterfield who continues to encourage and share her wisdom along the way. And for those other dear friends who pray and give their advice, thank you!

Most importantly, I express my gratefulness to my Lord and Savior, Jesus Christ. Without his grace, and most certainly, his infinite patience, there would be no Bible study. Thank you, Father, for sending your Son Jesus to us. Thank you, Jesus, for your example in righteous living which speaks so clearly through the ages. Thank you, Holy Spirit, for your help and encouragement every step of the way.

Table of Contents

Chapter One

Introduction to The Gospel of John

*A*re you familiar with the story of the blind men and the elephant? Four blind men are led to a massive bull elephant, positioned at different places around the elephant, and then asked to describe it. After a few minutes of poking and prodding the trunk, side, head, and legs, the men began to describe the elephant according to their experience.

"The elephant is long and flexible like a snake," said the one at the trunk.

"Oh, no. He is massive and sturdy with an span greater than my outstretched arms," stated the man at the elephant's side.

The third blind man who was holding one of the legs exclaimed, "You are both mistaken. He is round and solid like a tree trunk."

The fourth man at the elephant's head cried, "He has wings that flap like a bird!"

Who was right? Individually, each description was accurate, but each represented only a part of the total picture. No one account of the elephant was entirely complete. Combining all of their accounts was the only way to get an accurate picture of this mysterious animal called an elephant!

In a similar way, the four gospel accounts of the New Testament reflect the various viewpoints of each of their authors as they experienced Christ. The four gospels together relate the story of Christ from His annunciation to His resurrection. Each account has a different author. Each gospel provides a different focus. Each book reveals a unique perspective on Christ and His life.

The Word Became Flesh is a study of the fourth gospel, The Gospel of John. In the following chapters we will take a look at the culture, the people, and the Lord Jesus Christ as his life and ministry unfold before us. John's viewpoint is distinct from the other gospels for many reasons which we will discover over the course of our study. So, prepare to relate to Jesus Christ in new ways and even with a fresh understanding!

Whenever we begin to study the Bible, it is important to understand the *who, what, when, where,* and *why* of the passage. Who wrote the narrative? What was his purpose for writing it? What was the time frame, historical background, and geographical location for the writing? We will begin our study with some foundational elements that will help us to understand the full impact of John's gospel.

What is a "Gospel?"

As the apostles and other first generation Christians approached the end of their lives, they began to recognize a profound need for a lasting and accurate record of Christ. Four men, inspired by the Holy Spirit, preserved the historical and instructional Christian material by writing their perspective of the gospel story.

The Greek word for gospel is *euaggelion*, meaning the "telling of good news." In a number of languages the expression "the gospel" or "the good news" must be translated by a phrase. For example, "news that makes one happy" or "information that causes one joy" or "words that bring smiles" or "a message that causes the heart to be sweet."[1]

The four accounts contain proclamations and theological instructions for both a newly formed group of believers and those inquisitive about Jesus Christ. The gospels are not biographies because they do not include all of the details of Jesus' life. They are devoid of the normal biographical elements of character development, personality analysis, and intimate details of His personal life from childhood.

Although the gospels include many of the same details, they exclude countless events in the life of Christ. The gospels are unique in their character and message introducing a new genre of literature unlike any current Greco-Roman texts of its time.

The first three gospels, Matthew, Mark and Luke, are known as the Synoptic gospels. "Syn," meaning together and "opti" referring to the eye, characterize the common viewpoint of each of these narratives. Written in the middle of the first century and addressed primarily to first generation believers, these accounts include similar themes and stories in their text.

Matthew's gospel shows how the major events in the life of Jesus fulfill Old Testament prophecies. He depicts Jesus as the royal Messiah. Mark's gospel, believed to be the first written work, is an action account moving rapidly through the life of Christ. Luke is the only gospel author who is not a Jew. His gospel highlights the role of women, children, and the outcasts of society as they relate to Jesus.

The Gospel of John provides an entirely different point of view because of the author's time frame, audience, and purpose of his narrative. John probably recorded his gospel in the latter part of the first century and addressed second or even third generation Christians. John is not so concerned with the chronological events in the life of Jesus, the parables that he teaches, or in the miracles that He performs. Instead, his focus is upon the deeper spiritual truths that Christ reveals. John is combating the heretical doctrines that were beginning to seep into the developing church.

By selecting varying incidents in the life of Christ, John reinforces the practical truths of Christ's message. Through twenty-seven personal interviews, John spotlights people from different classes of society, at varying points of Jesus' ministry, and on different occasions. Jesus is characterized as the compassionate Son of God, able to relate to people from all walks of life and in a variety of circumstances.

In addition, John emphasizes the deity of Christ. By including seven supernatural signs, he demonstrates Jesus' authority over a particular earthly realm. He also reinforces the divinity of Christ through the seven "I AM" statements in the gospel and consistently employs certain words to illustrate spiritual truth. Some significant words that are frequently used in the gospel reinforce those themes: "light" is used twenty-one times;" life" thirty- five times; "love" thirty-one times; and "believe" ninety-eight times. John's gospel account is unique…92% of the information is not found in the other gospels.[2]

These early Christian authors wrote accurate details about the life of Christ for future generations. What greater message to proclaim than Jesus the Messiah, the founder of the kingdom of God!

    1. What is the focus of the gospel author in each of the following scriptures?

Matthew 1:1-17

Matthew 1:22, 2:23

Luke 1:1-4.

John 20:30-31

2. What comments does John include about his gospel in John 21:24-25?

3. The "good news" of the gospel is important to every generation, culture and people.

   A. Why is the message of Jesus Christ such "good news" to the people of His generation?

   B. What is the Apostle Paul's response to the gospel message according to Romans 1:15-17?

4. The various themes in the Gospel of John are found in the following verses. Describe the main idea or contrast of ideas shown in each passage.

   John 1:4-5

   John 3:15-16

   John 5:46-47

   John 10:29-30

   John 15:12

John: Disciple and Apostle

John and his brother James were engaged as Galilean fishermen in their father's business. On the invitation of Jesus, John left his former life and became a disciple of Christ. For the next three and a half years, John would live, eat, pray, minister, and walk alongside Christ as one of his closest companions. Eventually, John would come to be known as the "disciple whom the Lord loved."

Following the death and resurrection of Christ, the Apostle John rose to a position of prominence in the early church. At Jerusalem he helped to establish the church and approved of the evangelizing of Gentiles. He spent the later years of his life residing in Ephesus.

Polycrates, the bishop of Ephesus (190 A.D.), wrote that John who "reclined on the Lord's breast" after being "a witness and a teacher, fell asleep at Ephesus." Jerome also repeated the tradition that John lived to extreme old age. He recorded that when John had to be carried to Christian meetings, he would repeat again and again, "Little children, love one another."[3]

Although the author of this gospel is not mentioned by name, there is overwhelming historical evidence that the Apostle John wrote it. First, early church tradition attributes the authorship of the gospel to John. Irenaeus, an early church father, identified John as the writer of the fourth gospel recording it during Trajan's rule in Rome (98-117 A.D.). His source of information was Polycarp, a personal disciple of John.[4]

Second, there is internal evidence within the gospel itself. The author refers to "the disciple whom Jesus loved" and mentions other very personal matters that only an eyewitness would recount. Most scholars agree that John refers to himself in these instances.

The Apostle John authored four additional books in the New Testament. First, Second, and Third John bear his mark, as does the book of Revelation. Of the twelve original apostles, he becomes the most prolific writer.

According to Christian tradition, John is the only apostle who lives a long and fruitful life. Unlike the others who are martyred for the gospel message, John probably lives into the 2nd century A.D.

The Family of Zebedee

John's parents were Zebedee and Salome. The members of Zebedee's family were fishermen by trade and must have been successful in their trade for Zebedee employed servants. As the wife of Zebedee and mother of James and John. Salome sought places of honor in Christ's kingdom for her sons. She witnessed the crucifixion, and was present with the other women at the tomb. Matthew 27:56 names two women called Mary, and the mother of the sons of Zebedee at the cross. John 19:25 refers to two women called Mary, the mother of Jesus, and his mother's sister, who stood near the cross. If his mother's sister was Salome, then Jesus and John were cousins!

5. How does the Apostle John characterize himself in the following scriptures?

John 13:23

John 19:26-27

John 20:2, 8

6. Peter, James, and John are considered the "inner circle" of Jesus' disciples. On three

occasions they accompany Jesus when the other disciples do not. What happens in each instance?

Mark 5:37

Mark 9:2

Mark 14:33

What does this suggest about John?

7. During his lifetime, John experiences failure, triumph, and persecution. What qualities do you see displayed in the following scripture passages:

Luke 9:54-56

Acts 3:1-11

Acts 4:5-21

Acts 8:14-25

Galatians 2:9-10

Revelation 1:9

1 John 2:15-17

1 John 4:7-8

8. Examine 1 John 1:1-4, the introduction to the three books of John. What are the four ways John experiences the "good news" firsthand (verse 1)?

A.

B.

C.

D.

The Roman World

In the centuries before Christ's birth, the Roman Empire continued to rise in power enveloping nation by nation and bringing them under Rome's hand of authority. In 63 B.C. the Roman General Pompey conquered Syria and, consequently, Israel came under Roman rule. Herod the Great, half Jew and half Idumean, was given jurisdiction over Galilee and the rest of Judea.

Herod the Great ruled from 37 to 4 B.C. He was the most prolific builder that the region has ever known constructing palaces like Herodium, fortresses such as Masada, and a variety of cities. The Jewish temple, known as Herod's Temple, dominated the landscape of Jerusalem and occupied 1/6 of the city proper.

Despite his architectural brilliance, Herod was known for his brutality and paranoia. He overpowered the religious and political atmosphere in Jerusalem by executing 45 of the 70 members of the Jewish Sanhedrin. The ruling council opposed Herod and their penalty was death.

Herod also controlled the position of high priest of the temple during his reign. Herod had the power to appoint one priest, then for political or personal motives remove him from office either officially or by assassination. The position of high priest became a pawn in the hands of this Roman ruler.

Under this type of tyrannical rule, the Jews longed for the Messiah, the "Promised One" who would deliver them from the power of Rome. Many appeared proclaiming themselves as the Messiah and deceived others into following them. Although their efforts failed, the deception confused the people and tainted the reception of the true Son of God.

Israel's preconceived idea of the Messiah proved to be a stumbling block for many Jews. Their desire for a political deliverer clouded their acceptance of the One who will bring spiritual freedom to his people. The Kingdom of God would not be established externally on a national throne, but internally in the hearts of men and women.

Herod the Great

Despite his worldly success as an engineer and political figure, Herod's home life was disastrous. His first wife Miriam was charged with adultery and executed. Then followed nine additional wives and their offspring who took sides in the continuing battle for Herod's affections and power. At his death, Herod divided his realm between three of his sons: Herod Antipas was given Galilee and Peraea, Archelaus received Judea, Samaria, and Idumea, and Philip received the northeastern territories. Herod the Great ruled at the birth of Jesus and ordered the slaughter of the male infants; Herod Antipas, his son, reigned during the life, crucifixion, and resurrection of Jesus.

9. Herod's greatest achievement is the rebuilding of the temple in Jerusalem.

    A. According to John 2:20, how long is this new temple under construction?

    B. What is the ultimate future of Herod's temple predicted in Matthew 24:1-2

10. In stark contrast to his apparent generosity to the Jews, Herod the Great ruthlessly murdered anyone, real or imagined, who threatened his position as king. Matthew 2:1-18 illustrates Herod's true nature. What personality traits are displayed in this narrative?

Israel: A Conquered Nation

Date	*Event*
587 BC...Babylonian Empire	Jerusalem destroyed by King Nebuchadnezzar of Babylon
500-400 BC	Restoration of Jerusalem and the Temple (Ezra, Nehemiah)
176 BC	Maccabean Revolt...Judas Maccabee and sons lead rebellion
146 BC	Jewish Independence...Simon Maccabaeus becomes king and high priest...Hasmonean rule begins
63 BC	Pompey conquers Palestine
47 BC	Herod the Great becomes governor of Galilee...He is crowned "King of the Jews"
6 AD	Archaleus is removed from his position by Rome...Judea comes under direct Roman rule
7 AD	Judea is made a Roman imperial province
26 AD	Pilate arrives in Judea as the Roman governor
30 AD	John the Baptist begins his ministry Jesus is baptized by John the Baptist

Chapter Two
The Word Became Flesh

*E*very author understands that the success of their book rests in the first few pages. The opening of any book is critical and must grab the attention of the reader from the outset. John does not disappoint as he skillfully crafts an opening that explodes with a powerful spiritual message. Erasing any doubt concerning the nature of Christ, these first verses of his gospel herald the deity of Christ… Jesus is God!

> *In the beginning was the Word, and the Word was with God, and the Word was God. He was with God in the beginning. Through him all things were made; without him nothing was made that has been made. In him was life, and that life was the light of all mankind. The light shines in the darkness, and the darkness has not overcome it. (John 1:1-5)*

The prologue in verses John 1:1-18 provides a condensed overview of Jesus Christ the Messiah that will unfold throughout the rest of the gospel. John shows that Jesus is part of the triune Godhead, present at Creation. His purpose on earth is to reconcile humanity back to God and bring spiritual "sonship" to mankind. John also explains the importance of accepting Christ as the Messiah who came for all of mankind. This passage also introduces many of the major theological themes introduced in the Gospel of John. In this chapter of our study, we will take a few moments to examine some of the deeper concepts before we precede into the rest of the gospel.

In the first verse, we see that John's proclamation describes three different characteristics of the Word. The first, *In the beginning*, refers to the Word's presence at Creation…he was there. The second statement, *The Word was with God*, shows that the Word is separate from God yet equal to him. The Word has His own identity. The third statement, *The Word was God*, is a clear declaration of deity."[5] Jesus was the Word, present at Creation, and separate but equal to God!

John also chooses to use the familiar expression *logos* or the "Word" as he begins the gospel. To the Jew, *logos* meant the self-expression of God. It was through the word that God created the heavens and the earth. On the other hand, Greek reasoning held that *logos* was a rational principle that accounted for the beauty and order of creation.[6] In using this specific word, John captures the interest and attention of both Jew and Greek inviting them to read on.

John's opening of the gospel also refutes the prevailing heresies of his day. Gnosticism had become a new intellectual approach to religion, mixing Christianity with mostly Greek beliefs. Gnosticism comes from the Greek word *gnosis*, which meant knowledge. It built upon heresy and Greek philosophy that stressed all matter was evil but spirit was good. This being the case, gnostics believed God could not have created the material world because of its evil nature. Their beliefs rejected the idea that God could appear, or even would choose to appear in corrupt flesh. John's statement that *Christ became flesh and made his dwelling among us* served as a polemic, or argument against these Greek philosophical ideas that are especially prevalent at this time.

Gnosticism

Gnostic beliefs were a stumbling block to true faith in Christ. There were two differing viewpoints in gnostic thought. One view held that because matter was evil, Jesus could not have actually come in human form. He only "appeared" in human form and only "appeared" to suffer. The other view suggested that the divine Logos came upon the human Jesus and departed prior to the crucifixion. Therefore, the deity of Christ was never crucified.

Salvation was also philosophical to the Gnostics: it was a special "knowing" of the truth, which was imparted only to special people through initiation. Sin and evil were associated with ignorance or lack of knowledge.[7] Gnosticism plagued early Christianity. It challenged the early church father's message, even creeping into the teachings of the church.

1.Read John 1:1-3 and 14.

A. What distinctive qualities can you attribute to the "Word" in verses 1, 2, and 14?

B. According to John 1:3, what role did the "Word" play in creation?

C. What title is used in Revelation 19:13 for Jesus?

D. Who is the Word?

2. Compare John 1:1-5 with the original account of creation in Genesis 1:1-5. What similarities do you see in both of the these passages?

Christ the Light

While on vacation in the Midwest, my family and I took a guided tour of a famous local cavern. As we wound our way down into the belly of the cave, our guide led the way by scattering light from his flashlight. When we reached the bottom of the cave, we entered into a large expansive opening. We paused as our guide asked us to remain still. Then he turned off his flashlight.

There are no words to describe the eeriness and overwhelming feeling of helplessness we experienced. All reference points were swallowed in the darkness—any sense of direction disappeared and we were paralyzed in silence.

Then suddenly our seasoned guide turned his flashlight back on, and the craggy rock formation was bathed in shadowy light. Amidst the nervous sighs of relief and raised eyebrows, we continued our journey onward. Just one minuscule flashlight illuminated the entire cavern.

In a similar way, Jesus came into the world as a spiritual light to illuminate our sinful darkness. Without His guiding light, we stumble in our own spiritual darkness lacking direction and purpose. He is our light that directs and leads us onto a righteous path.

John introduces this concept of "light versus darkness" at the outset of his gospel. It will continue as a dominant theme throughout his writing.

Light

In the Bible, light is a symbol of God. God spoke "Let there be light" and creation began. God is described as covering himself with light as with a garment. His countenance is light. His written word is described as "a lamp to my feet and a light to my path." At the end of Revelation, the Lord God is said to be the "light of his servants." The New Testament proclaims Christ as the light of the world who calls people "out of darkness into his marvelous light."

3. A common theme throughout John's gospel is the concept of light and darkness. What are the distinguishing characteristics of this "light" according to the following scriptures?

    A. John 1:4

    B. John 1:5

    C. John 1:9

4. The author John uses an interesting Greek verb, *katalambano*, in verse five for the word overcome. The word can be translated to understand[8] or to gain control over, to overcome, to gain control of as in *and the darkness did not gain control over it.*[9]

    A. What can darkness not overcome?

    B. What is the darkness this scripture refers to?

Christ in the World

John 1:10-13

Imagine heaven as it anticipates the incarnation of Christ. The Father has waited thousands of years watching His creation struggling defenseless against the tyranny of sin. God's plan is unfolding—His Son will walk among creation and show them the Father's true nature. Sin will be defeated. Fellowship with God will be restored. As the angel's divine chorus echoes upon Bethlehem's hills heralding the birth of The Word, all of heaven anxiously awaits.

Now imagine the hardened truth of the world's response. How is the Son of God welcomed? Where is the celebration worthy of his visitation? Even those who are called by His name, follow His law, and serve God in His temple are blind to His appearance. The Lord of Life appears to bring a new spiritual birth to His creation, but He is, for the most part, ignored.

Born of God (John 1:13)

The new birth through Christ is a unique process. First, it is not like a natural act that brings people into the world—not of "natural descent" (literally, bloods), suggesting the combining of mother and fathers genes . Second, the new birth is not related to "human decision" or the natural, human desire for children. Third, spiritual rebirth is not a result of a "husband's will," suggesting the special desire to carry on a family name.

So, the new birth is something supernatural, a work of God in regeneration. A person **perceives** *Jesus as the Son of God who came to take away the sins of the world. He or she* **receives** *Jesus as the Son of God, and* **believes** *totally and completely in that truth.*[10] *This is the sole basis for becoming a child of God.*

5. In verses 10-12 there are three different Greek verbs that reflect how we may interact with Christ.

A. In verse 10, *ginosko*, to know, understand, to perceive,[11] is the Greek word for recognize. What was the reaction of the world to the Messiah?

B. In verse 11 and 12, the second verb is receive (*paralambano or lambano*). This word indicates a joining to one's self, acceptance or acknowledgment.[12] What was the response to Christ?

C. According to verse 12, the last verb in this passage is *pisteuo* meaning to think to be true, to be persuaded of, to credit, place confidence in[13] for the word believe. What was necessary to become a son of God? What does Jesus give to those who believe in Him?

D. Perceive, Receive, and Believe. How are these three words crucial to being "born of God?"

Christ's Glory Revealed

John 1:14-18

Although the world may not have recognized or received the Son of God, John's response to Christ is quite different. He has personally witnessed the glory of the Son of God firsthand as he lived daily at Jesus' side. John experienced this divine nature of Christ through his teachings, his ministry and example. His testimony of Christ is a jubilant reaction to the Messiah he has come to know, trust, and love.

In verse fourteen, John also describes Jesus as being full of grace and truth. Reading further in verse seventeen, John explains that the law was given through Moses; grace and truth came through Jesus Christ (John 1:17). Moses brought righteousness through the law of God fifteen hundred years earlier, but Jesus is introducing a higher order of truth and a new spiritual concept…grace.

Grace comes from the Greek word *charis*, a word reflecting joy, pleasure, delight, good will, loving-kindness, or favor.[14] More specifically, it is the unearned and even undeserved merciful kindness which God extends to mankind. Grace can be summarized in the following:

God's

Riches

At

Christ's

Expense

Jesus was full of grace and truth. His words and actions will transform the lives of thousands in his day and billions throughout history. Grace simply demonstrates the mercy and compassion of God as humanity receives this precious free gift.

The Grace of God

The idea of grace is very prominent in the New Testament. Jesus says that he came to seek and save the lost. Many of his parables teach the doctrine of grace. The parable of the laborers in the vineyard teaches that God is answerable to no one for his gifts of grace. The prodigal son was welcomed by his father in a way he did not deserve. The parable of the great supper shows that spiritual privilege does not ensure final bliss, and that the gospel invitation is to all.[15]

6. In John 1:14, a key scripture for the introduction, the author makes some definitive statements about Jesus. The Greek word *skenoo*, to dwell, actually means tabernacled or pitched his tent. The word alludes to the tabernacle where the Shekinah or manifested glory of the Lord appeared in the Old Testament. It also refers to God's permanent dwelling among His people in the book of Revelation.[16] List John's observations about Christ.

7. In what particular ways do you think John experienced the glory of God? How does today's Christian experience the glory of God?

8. John calls Jesus the "One and Only" both in verse 14 and 18. How is this statement important

for us today, as well as people of Biblical times?

Making it Personal

How important is a word? In Genesis, God created the world with his words. John wrote of how Christ as The Word was present during creation and continues to generate new life in those who believe in him. Words have power.

But think about it...doesn't everything actually start with a word? Whether an idea, a vision, or an invention, all things are created by the words that we speak. We think, we speak, and we act on those words. God has given us the power to craft our environment through the veracity and power of our words. Whatever we accept as truth, whatever we deem possible, all things begin with a word.

In the first few verses of The Gospel of John, we have examined the life-changing message of God's word. Jesus is eternal and Creator of the universe. He came to dwell with us to demonstrate the divine nature of the Father. He fulfilled the plan of salvation by becoming human and dying for the sins of mankind. Belief in Jesus brings spiritual renewal or a "new birth."

For many, these are familiar truths. But for some, these truths are new or perhaps you are seeing them with fresh spiritual eyes. As you reflect upon this chapter, take the time to contemplate your own spiritual condition.

9. Ask yourself the following questions:

A. Who is Jesus Christ to you?

B. How has your belief or lack of belief in Him influenced your life?

C. Jesus was "full" of grace and truth and we have received from the fullness of His grace. In what specific ways have you been blessed by God's grace and truth in your life?

10. Each of us can experience God's freedom through grace. Is there an area of your life that needs the grace of God, His divine nature and unmerited favor? Ask for His help.

The Bible states:

> *If you declare with your mouth, "Jesus is Lord," and believe in your heart that God raised him from the dead, you will be saved. For it is with your heart that you believe and are justified, and it is with your mouth that you profess your faith and are saved. Romans 10:9-10*

The following prayer is a reaffirmation of faith in Jesus Christ as the Son of God. For some, this will be your first time to pray in this manner. You are choosing to accept Christ as your personal Savior. This simple prayer will begin your "new birth" experience.

Jesus,

I believe you are Lord, Creator, and the one and only Son of God. Because you came to earth as a man and died for my sins, I can be forgiven and experience a spiritual "new birth." I receive you, Jesus, as my Lord and Savior. Please wash away the affects of my mistakes, failures, and wrongdoings. Help me to experience the fullness of your grace as I walk in your truth. Thank you, Jesus. Amen.

Notes

Chapter Three
A Voice In the Wilderness

*I*t was a chilly December day in Galilee. Robed in white and shivering alongside the murky waters of the river, my family waited our turn to experience what would be the highlight of our trip to Israel…water baptism in the River Jordan! Yes, it was cold. But we overcame the coolness of the air with the rising warmth and conviction in our heart. Like so many who had passed this way before us, my family was making a public statement. We were not only confirming our faith in the swirling waters of the Jordan, but we were openly testifying to our beliefs. The water was freezing, but we were willing to suffer the momentary discomfort. We were declaring our faith and following in the footsteps of Christ!

As The Gospel of John continues, the author introduces two central Biblical concepts—the witness and their corresponding testimony of belief. Throughout the gospel, John will continually highlight various people as they share their testimony about Christ, the Father, and other important aspects of the account.

Although we consider personal testimonies as characteristic of the New Testament, God inspired many in the Old Testament to carry his message. He chose the Jewish nation to experience this unique relationship with him. God sent his messangers to other nations and individuals who would receive his righteous message. Abraham, Joseph, and Moses were key figures in the narrative of Egypt. Rahab the harlot from Jericho heard of the Israelites and her heart was turned toward God. Esther intervened for her people at a critical time in the midst of Persia. Jonah was sent to Nineveh to offer a message of repentance to a bloodthirsty, brutal people. As a result of a Jewish serving girl's witness, Naman the Syrian traveled to Israel to receive his healing from leprosy.

In the New Testament, the concept of witnessing or giving a testimony becomes a central theme. Bible dictionaries indicate two distinctions of the word "witness." First, a witness is a **person** *(marturia)*, like a prophet, who testifies concerning future events. Second, a witness is an **action** *(martureo)*. It means to affirm what one has seen or heard or experienced, or what he knows by divine revelation or inspiration.[17] Through actions, words, and by their very presence, New Testament believers are called to be witnesses of the gospel message.

John the Baptist: Witness of Christ
John 1:19-28

John the Baptist is the first recorded witness of Christ in this gospel. As a prophet and forerunner to Christ, his entire life bears the thumb print of God. In Luke 1:5-80, we can read of his supernatural conception, God's divine purpose, and his relationship to Jesus. Through an angelic visitation, his priestly father Zacharias receives the announcement that *John will bring joy and gladness and many will rejoice at his birth*. John will be *great in the sight of the Lord; filled with the Holy Spirit in the womb*. He will *turn people to the Lord in the spirit and power of Elijah*.

As God's prophet, John the Baptist embarks on a divine mission. He calls people to repentance and prepares their hearts to receive the Messiah. However, his ministry lacks approval from the religious authority in Jerusalem. News had reached the capitol city of his unique baptism and the swelling reaction from the common people had become a concern.

Two distinct groups, Levites and priests, are sent from the religious hierarchy in Jerusalem to investigate the nature of John's activities. The priests represent the theological authorities of the nation. The Levites, descendants of the tribe of Levi, are concerned with the ritual and service of the temple. Their motivation..."Who are you? What right do you have to perform this religious rite outside of Jerusalem?" According to biblical prophecy and tradition, the Jews expected Elijah to return with the Messiah (Malachi 4:5). They also anticipated a Prophet who would be like Moses (Deuteronomy 18:15). Did John the Baptist claim to be one of these?

This is probably an unofficial inquiry, a kind of fact-finding assignment to satisfy the curiosity of the Sanhedrin, the Jewish religious council. A part of John's witness includes an open confession to the religious establishment in John 1:20.

 The word "Jews" used in John 1:19 is a term the author uses throughout this gospel to distinguish the Jerusalem religious structure who opposed him. The Apostle John uses this word as a distinctive label to differentiate the leaders of Judaism from the common Jewish population.

The Prophet

A Prophet was a person who served as a divine channel of communication between God and man. The biblical prophets played a crucial role in the development of Judaism and Christianity. They were regarded as predictors of the future, whose words pointed to the coming of Jesus and to the future course of world history. Prophets were considered moral and ethical innovators, bringing Israelite religion to a higher level of development.

There are five titles for the men and women of the Old Testament who served as prophets. The most common title used is "prophet," from the Hebrew word meaning "one who calls" or "one who is called." Another designation for prophetic figures is "visionary," a title that refers to the distinctive means by which these individuals received their revelations. Samuel was called a "seer," a specialist in communicating with God through visions, dreams, or divination. The title "man of God," was frequently used and appears particularly in the prophetic stories set in the time of Elijah and Elisha. During the same period, the writers of Kings speak of prophetic groups called "sons of the prophets." Various types of prophets existed in Israel, and individual prophets had characteristics unique unto themselves.[18]

1. In order to be a reliable witness, John grew to realize who he was and who he was not. According to these scriptures, who was John the Baptist?

John 1:6-7

John 1:19-21

2. John the Baptist frames his identity in reference to Jesus with three powerful declarations. As you read each verse, describe how John viewed himself in respect to Jesus.

John 1:15

John 1:23

John 1:27

John 1:29-34

John the Baptist has received a special mandate from God. He is to lead the people to repentance through water baptism and reveal the Messiah to Israel. One day on the banks of the river Jordan, John fulfills his purpose. As Jesus approaches him, John testifies prophetically... *Look, the Lamb of God, who takes away the sin of the world!* John's witness continues with his testimony of Christ's baptism and the affirmation of the Holy Spirit. He concludes with an emphatic declaration *This is the Son of God.*

Baptism

There were four different baptisms known to the Israelites at this juncture in time. They were:

1. Jewish ceremonial washings dictated by law.

2. Qumran purification rites that applied to a religious sect known as the Essenes.

3. Proselyte baptism for a new Jewish convert.

4. The baptism of John that was primarily a baptism of repentance.

John's baptism probably followed the pattern of proselyte baptism requiring a renunciation of evil, complete immersion in water, and then reclothing as a member of the holy community.[19] By accepting baptism at John's hands the people were expressing their repentance and their desire for forgiveness. Water baptism was also a preparatory and symbolical act: it prepared the person for the ministry of the Coming One, Jesus Christ, the Messiah.[20]

3. John the Baptist announced Jesus as the Lamb of God. How do these scriptures clarify that title?

Genesis 22:7-8

Exodus 12:3-11

Isaiah 53:7

4. John the Baptist is sent from God and possesses a divine revelation about the Messiah. He does not know who the Messiah is (verse 31), but God has given him insight into discerning the Christ. What particular act identifies Jesus as the promised Messiah?

John 3:22-36

John the Baptist faces a pressing problem, a struggle that can still plague even the best of us. John has preached repentance to Israel and baptized those who have recognized their spiritual shortcomings. But, now the main thrust of his ministry is waning—the Messiah has been revealed to Israel and is growing in popularity. Jesus and His disciples are baptizing and their crowds are larger than John's. Some of his disciples actually leave him to follow Jesus. The remaining loyal disciples are concerned and they question John for an explanation. His response is a model of humility and self-awareness. His reaction demonstrates a deep and abiding maturity in God. John has endeavored relentlessly in the ministry God has given him. The time has come for the greater one to take center stage.

5. John continues to testify concerning himself, his role, and the relationship he has to Christ. What does he have to say about himself and his relationship to Jesus in the following verses?

A. John 3:27

B. John 3:29

C. John 3:30

Beyond the Gospels

John plays a vital role in preparing Israel for her redeemer. The fact that Herod considered it necessary to have John killed demonstrates his importance. Years after Jesus' death, Christian missionaries still encounter people in Asia Minor who know only the baptism of John. The far-reaching effects from John the Baptist's ministry is found in Acts, where on two occasions Christians encounter disciples of John. After being further instructed, they are received into the church (Priscilla and Aquila meet Apollos in Acts 18:24-28, and Paul meets twelve such disciples, perhaps associated with Apollos, in Acts 19:1-7).[21]

The Disciples Witness

John 1:35-51

In this passage of scripture, we will meet the first disciples. A disciple is a term for one who is a "learner" or follows another's teachings. He was a pupil of a teacher and a familiar sight with a rabbi from whom he learned traditional lore. Jesus and John the Baptist were not officially recognized as teachers by the religious system, but they were popularly known as a teacher or rabbi, and their associates were known as disciples. The word "disciple" can be used of all who responded to their message, but it can also refer more narrowly to those who accompanied Jesus on his travels, and especially to the twelve apostles.

Jesus based discipleship on a call. It involved personal allegiance to him, following him, and giving him an exclusive loyalty. In at least some cases, it meant literal abandonment of home, business ties and possessions. But in every case readiness to put the claims of Jesus first, whatever the cost. Such an attitude went well beyond the normal pupil-teacher relationship and gave the word "disciple" a new meaning.

The responsibilities of disciples included preaching his message, casting out demons and healing the sick. Although these were primarily delegated to the Twelve, they were not confined to them. Those who became disciples were taught by Jesus and appointed as his representatives.[22]

In this section, John the Baptist declares Jesus as the "Lamb of God" and two of his disciples follow Jesus for further inquiry. These first disciples respond to Jesus as Messiah with a subsequent witness about him. It is not enough to merely receive the Messiah. Something within them prompts the disciples to spread the "good news" that the true Christ has come into their midst.

"Jesus, Christ, and Messiah"

What is the difference between the names "Jesus," "Messiah," and "Christ?" Jesus is actually a Greek translation of His personal name, much like Jeffrey or Margaret. In Hebrew His proper name was **Joshua** *meaning "Yahweh is salvation," a name given to Jesus by his parents Mary and Joseph. Because the New Testament was written in Greek, Joshua became Jesus in the written text.*

The title Messiah"comes from the Hebrew word **mashach**, *which signifies a ceremonial anointing in the Old Testament. Kings, priests, and sometimes prophets were anointed for divine service in their respective office. Therefore, Jesus is the anointed one, the Messiah.*

The name Christ or **Christos** *in Greek, is the translation of the Hebrew word rendered Messiah. It occurs five hundred and fourteen times in the New Testament. It denotes that he was anointed or consecrated to his great redemptive work as Prophet, Priest, and King of his people.[23]*

6. John the Baptist taught numerous disciples who worked alongside of him. Two of these disciples decide to follow Jesus. One is unnamed (most believe this is the author John).

   A. Who is the first named disciple in John's gospel to follow Jesus?

   B. What has led them to leave John and follow another?

   C. How did they demonstrate their eagerness to become disciples (verse 39)?

D. Within the final twelve disciples, there were two sets of brothers—James and John, and Peter and Andrew, often referred to as Andrew, the Bringer. What was the first thing Andrew did after spending the day with Jesus (verse 41)?

7. In verse 43 Jesus beckons Phillip as the fourth disciple to follow him.

A. What is Phillip's first reaction to being called?

B. Nathanael is *under the fig tree* when Jesus first sees him. *Under the fig tree* is a Jewish phrase describing meditation on the Law of Moses.[24] Apparently, Nathanael is a student of the Old Testament and familiar with the Law and the Prophetic literature of Judaism. How does Philip appeal to Nathanael in his testimony of Jesus (verse 45)?

C. What does Jesus promise to Nathanael and his disciples in John 1:50?

8. The disciples use a number of titles which testify about Jesus in this scripture segment (John 1:35-50). List the different designations that describe Jesus.

A Divine Witness of Jesus
John 5:31-40, John 8:12-19

If a witness takes the stand in the United States, puts her hand on a Bible, and "swears to tell the truth, the whole truth, and nothing but the truth," her testimony is accepted. However, in the first century A.D., Jewish law prohibits a man testifying in his own behalf. His own words are not valid as an acceptable testimony. Instead, two witnesses must agree for the testimony to be recognized as truth.

In this portion of the Gospel of John, the Jews in Jerusalem confront Jesus because he has healed an invalid on the Sabbath. Jesus testifies about himself on this occasion, but because of Jewish law he points out additional testimonies which validate and confirm he is the divine Son of God.

9. In John 5:31-40, what are the four additional witnesses that Jesus mentions?

A.

B.

C.

D.

E. According to John 5:37-38, why don't the Jews accept the testimony of the Father?

10. There are two levels of validation for Jesus. One is worldly acceptance and the other is divine approval. On the human level, Jesus is measured by earthly qualifications and expectations. The higher second level appeals to his divine purpose in the eyes of God. How does Jesus testify about himself in these scriptures? Does he satisfy human standards and ideals or does he answer to a higher calling and accountability?

A. John 5:31

B. John 8:12-19

C. Revelation 3:14

Rabbi

*The original Hebrew word, **rab**, meant "great," and came to be used for a person in a respected position. **Rabbi**, "my great one," was used as a reverential form of address. By the end of the 2nd century B.C. the word **rab** was used for a teacher, and **rabbi** as the respectful address, "my teacher."*

*In New Testament times, the word was a title of honor, applied once to John the Baptist and twelve times to our Lord. In Matthew 23:7, in contrast to the scribes' delight in being called **rabbi**, the disciples are told not to be so called—"for you have one teacher…and you are all brethren." **Rabboni** is a heightened form of **rabbi** used to address the Lord in Mark 10:51 and John 20:16.*

The word "rabbi" came to be used as the title of the authorized teachers of the Law; in modern Judaism, it is used for those who are ordained to this work.[25]

Making it Personal

Think of what first brought you to Christ—was it a friend who shared her life as a Christian? A loving gesture extended toward you personally? Perhaps a timely remark caught your attention and caused you to begin to search for ultimate truth?

My encounter with Christianity came through my neighbor who was committed to sharing the love of God. Her loving, joyful witness became the key that unlocked the door to my heart. Sandy stirred a hunger within me for the unexplained peace that characterized her own life. Here is my testimony:

Many years ago, as a twenty-nine year old mother, I found myself completely overwhelmed at the prospect of being pregnant once again. In contrast, my congenial neighbor, the mother of three rambunctious boys, maintained a positive, compassionate outlook on life. What was her secret? Surely no one could be that happy with so much chaos surrounding her!

My curiosity was awakened and I began to prod her with pointed and provoking questions. As the months passed, she taught me about the grace of God and His loving, forgiving nature. Through her prayers and perseverance, much like Andrew and Philip, I "found" the Messiah.

Over thirty years have passed since that glorious moment of salvation, but God's faithfulness has never left me. When my father's suicide shattered our family, the inexplicable peace of God encompassed my devastated soul. During my mother's debilitating illness, He provided wisdom and grace to make the difficult decisions and stabilize sibling upheaval. In the down times, in the weak moments, when strength failed and hope was bleak, God was a constant beacon of light. Through the highs and the lows, the peaks and valleys, God has proven Himself to be ever faithful in my life.

As we continue in our study of the witness, consider how powerful words and actions are to those in your community. Like Phillip and Andrew, there are people in your sphere of influence who can be affected by your testimony of Christ.

11. In Luke 24:48 Jesus declares to His disciples, "You are witnesses of these things."

   A. What is required to be a successful witness for Christ?

   B. How have you already been a positive witness for Christ?

   C. Take a moment to reflect and record what God has already done in your life.

12. List the names of a few people in your life who need to hear the "good news" of the gospel of Christ. How could you begin to testify about Christ to them? Pray and ask him to help you reach out to others.

   Lord Jesus,

   Truly, you are a great and wonderful Savior. Thank you for your many blessings and your faithfulness in my life. Please help me to share your goodness and truth with others. Let me be sensitive to the heart-felt needs of my family and community. I commit myself to become a vibrant and effective witness for you. Amen

Notes

Chapter Four

Close Encounters of the Divine Kind

*W*hen life begins to unravel like a ball of wayward yarn, I long to find sanctuary in the arms of Jesus. I imagine myself entwined around his powerful frame with my head resting peacefully upon his shoulder. Ahhh…nestling like a distressed child seeking comfort and assurance. Surely, in his arms I will discover the solace that I so desperately seek.

What would it be like to have an intimate, personal conversation with the God of the universe? How wonderful to ask him those nagging, unanswered questions. And to discuss the "ins and outs" of the world with the Creator himself. What a glorious experience! But a close encounter with Jesus would not be a one-way conversation. As the omniscient, shepherd of my soul he would not be a passive participant. Jesus might have some direct, probing questions of His own.

The public phase of Jesus' ministry is ready to begin. John highlights the interactions between Jesus and a variety of individuals. These wide-ranging dialogues include people from all walks of life, both Jew and Gentile, and of high and low position in society. As one of the inner circle of disciples, the Apostle John must have been privy to these conversations or perhaps Jesus spoke freely with His disciples about them.

John depicts Jesus as the compassionate, concerned Son of God who takes the time to converse one-on-one with a variety of people. Men and women are transformed by his glory. The learned Pharisee Nicodemus, the outcast Samaritan woman, and even the woman caught in adultery are drawn to his goodness.

Jesus is the Savior who ministers to the masses, but he is also the Redeemer who cares about the individual. The author addresses some of the most controversial subjects of his day, as Jesus comes together with both the respected and rejected members of society. He encounters men and women from all walks of life as no one is beyond the scope of his concern.

Cleansing the Temple
John 2:13-25

In the Gospel of John, Jesus travels to Jerusalem on four different occasions, all celebrations of Jewish feasts. The Law of Moses mandates all males to make a pilgrimage to Jerusalem on three separate occasions during the year—Passover in the spring, Pentecost in the early summer, and the Feast of Tabernacles in the fall. John records Jesus' first visit at the beginning of his ministry during the Feast of Passover. The second visit occurs during an unknown feast, perhaps the Feast of Tabernacles. The third journey is for the Feast of Tabernacles and the fourth and final visitation is the celebration of Passover.

In this first visit, Jesus and his disciples travel from the rural seaside community of Galilee to the cosmopolitan city of Jerusalem. It was the first month of the Jewish year, the month of Abib, and in accordance with Jewish law, the men make the journey to Jerusalem's temple for Passover (Exodus 12:1-20). He begins his public ministry by performing miraculous signs among the people. But the corruption that confronts Jesus in the Temple courts stirs a righteous anger within him. He surges into action!

The zeal of the Son of God for his Father's house brings a quick response from the Jewish leaders. As they confront Jesus, they want to know one question...where does he get his authority to do these acts? They demand a "sign," a special miracle to prove himself. Essentially, they are asking Jesus for his credentials. Where was he taught? Who was his teacher? Did he meet their standards of academic training? Somehow, they missed the greater message of salvation and were more concerned with formal proof of his qualifications.

Temple Transactions

At each of the annual religious events, the moneychangers stood to profit greatly. As the Jewish populace traveled from near and far, many came from outlying foreign areas. Each Jew and proselyte—women, slaves, and minors excluded— had to pay a temple tribute of one-half shekel. Foreign coinage was exchanged for the acceptable temple currency. In addition, a fee would be charged for the transfer, especially if the amount was in excess of the required temple tribute.

Another type of offering, a sacrificial animal, was also available for purchase. Many pilgrims brought their own sacrifices, but the remainder purchased their animals in Jerusalem. Each animal had to meet high purity standards to be considered appropriate for sacrifice. Because of this many purchased the animal within the temple to assure its purity.

At the time of Christ, the "Temple Bazaar" was the property and principal source of income for the sons of Annas, the High Priest. The Rabbis and Josephus, a Jewish historian, recorded the greed and corruption of this infamous high-priestly family. It is no wonder that Jesus denounced the Temple-market as a den of robbers.[26]

1. The word zeal or *zelos* in verse 17, is defined as an excitement of mind, ardor, fervor of spirit; an ardor in embracing, pursuing, or defending anything; the fierceness of indignation or punitive zeal.[27] The disciples recall the words of Psalm 69:9, *Zeal for your house will consume me.*

    A. How does Jesus view the Temple (verse 16)?

    B. What is Jesus' reaction to the corruption within the place of worship?

    C. How does this zeal prompt him into action?

2. The Jewish leaders demand a sign from Jesus to demonstrate where He has received his authority.

    A. How does Jesus respond to the question from the Jewish authorities?

    B. How do the religious authorities respond?

C. In verse 23, note the reaction of the common people.

D. How do the disciples react in verse 22?

E. Jesus mentions one kind of temple and the Jews discuss another. How do they compare to each other? Consider the type of temple, the builder, and longevity.

Herod's Temple

The temple erected by the exiles on their return from Babylon had stood for about five hundred years. The building had suffered from natural decay as well as from the assaults of hostile armies. Herod the Great, wanting to gain the favor of the Jews, proposed to rebuild it and the work was begun in 18 B.C. It was carried out at great labor and expense, and on a scale of surpassing splendor. The main part of the building was completed in ten years, but the temple was finally completed in 65 A.D.

Herod's Temple had two courts. One was intended for the Israelites only. The other, a large outer court called "the court of the Gentiles," was used by strangers of all nations. The court of the Gentiles housed the market area for the Temple. It was here that the moneychangers and animal merchants transacted their business.

Within forty years after the Lord's crucifixion, his prediction of its overthrow was accomplished. The Roman legions took the city of Jerusalem by storm in 70 A.D. Despite the strenuous efforts Titus made to preserve the temple, his soldiers set fire to it in several places. It was utterly destroyed and never rebuilt.[28]

Nicodemus: Born of the Spirit

(John 3:1-21)

Nicodemus was a conservative Pharisee, a teacher of Israel, and a member of the Sanhedrin. He is only mentioned in John, and plays an important role in representing the Jewish leaders that were favorable toward Jesus. However, many still wrestled with their public confession of Jesus as the Christ.

As a Pharisee, Nicodemus lived by the strictest possible religious rules. This passage indicates that he was deeply sincere in his quest for truth. He approaches Jesus after witnessing his miracles at the Temple and comes with an open curiosity to speak freely with the Messiah.

Nicodemus comes by night, not because he is afraid of being seen, but most likely because he wants to have a quiet, uninterrupted conversation with the new Teacher *come from God*. The fact that Nicodemus uses the plural pronoun "we," and Jesus responds with the plural "you" may indicate that Nicodemus represents the religious leaders.[29] As a prominent teacher of the law, Jesus questions him directly and challenges Nicodemus to receive a greater revelation.

Perhaps the most quoted scripture of the New Testament is *For God so loved the world that he gave his one and only Son, that whoever believes in him shall not perish but have eternal life*. Whether this profound statement is a continuation of the conversation between Jesus and Nicodemus or the author John's commentary, it shines brightly with the truth of God's salvation. This is the essence of the gospel message—the love of God, belief in his Son, and the promise of eternal life.

3. In the evening, Nicodemus comes to Jesus in order to discuss the events of the day. What does Nicodemus already believe about Jesus as he comes to speak with Him (John 3:2)?

4. Jesus introduces a new concept to the learned teacher, that of being "born again." To be *born from above* means a transformation of a person so that he is able to enter another world and adapt to its conditions.[30] Jesus instructs Nicodemus on the two types of birth—the birth of water and the birth of spirit. To enter the kingdom of God, man must be born of both.

A. In verse 3, Jesus describes the importance of the "born again" experience. What are his words to Nicodemus?

B. Nicodemus is confused by Jesus' words. To what does he think Jesus refers?

C. How do these scriptures further explain spiritual birth?

Titus 3:5

1 Peter 1:23

5. The evening breeze gently blows and cools the city as a backdrop to their conversation. Wind is one of the symbols of the Spirit of God in the Bible and can be translated as spirit in both Greek and Hebrew. Like the wind, the Spirit is invisible but powerful; and unexplainable and unpredictable.[31] What further insight does 1 Corinthians 2:14-16 provide about the role of the Holy Spirit?

6. In John 3:16-21, the author presents the gospel message in a few short verses.

A. The word love (*agapao*) is used in verse 16. It means to welcome, entertain, be fond of, love dearly, to be well pleased or contented at or with a thing.[32] What kind of love characterizes God?

B. God's desire is to give eternal life to all who ask. He does not want any to perish (*apollumi*) meaning to perish, to destroy, to be lost or ruined.[33] In verse 16, what does God offer as an alternative to perishing?

C. The word condemn (*krino*) is used three times in verses 17 and 18. In verse 19 it is translated as verdict. The word means to determine, resolve, decree, to judge or to pronounce an opinion concerning right and wrong.[34]

How do we escape condemnation (verse 18)?

According to verse 19, what condemnation or verdict is upon the world?

Sozo

The Greek word **sozo** *(to save) encompasses the total act of salvation. It is not just a decision that promises eternal life, but the many facets of salvation that include so much more.*

First, it carries the message of wholeness...body, mind, soul, and spirit. Second, "sozo" also means to keep safe and sound and to rescue from danger or destruction. Third, salvation affects our physical body having the connotation of saving one suffering from disease, to make well and restore to health. Finally, **sozo** *in its strictest sense, means to deliver us from the penalties of Messianic judgment.*

So, salvation affects more than our spirit. It is the act of a loving God who designed salvation to touch every aspect of our life.[35]

The Woman at the Well

John 4:1-42

As Jesus and his disciples leave the province of Judea, they choose one of three possible roads to Galilee: 1) along the coast 2) across the Jordan and up through Perea or 3) the shortest route straight through Samaria. Prejudice against the mixed race of Samaritans made this route the least favorable for Jews. Jesus is about to shatter the boundaries of gender and race.

Weary and thirsty from travel, he pauses to rest at the sixth hour (around noon on the Hebrew timetable) about a half-mile from the city of Sychar. The ancient, carved limestone well of Jacob offers a place of refreshment from their fatiguing journey. John does not falter in depicting Jesus in His frail humanity. He is tired, thirsty, and hungry.

When a Samaritan woman approaches the well, he engages her in a conversation. Although it was not acceptable for a man, and especially a Rabbi, to speak with a woman in public, Jesus breaks the social barrier and interacts with the Samaritan woman.

Requesting water from the well, he, in return, is prepared to give her the covenant water of eternal life. Jesus confronts her past with blatant honesty. She has had many husbands and Jesus addresses her current ungodly lifestyle. She is living with a man not her husband. This could be the reason she is alone at the well in the middle of the day.

The mercy of Christ doesn't condemn her, instead, he corrects her spiritual errors. Finally, Jesus offers the Samaritan woman hope. True worship will no longer depend upon a physical site, but be available to anyone who will worship the Father in spirit and truth.

The disciples return only to discover their Master is deep in conversation with the Samaritan woman. Apparently, they have learned not to question his behavior, even though he is violating Jewish social etiquette. Jesus' love for mankind and desire to preach the kingdom of God proves far greater than any obstacle of man's design. His one focus is to do the will of the Father.

The Samaritans

The Samaritans took their name from the city of Samaria, the capital of the Northern Kingdom of Israel from the time of the kings Omri and Ahab. The Assyrians destroyed the city of Samaria in 721 B.C. About twenty–seven thousand people of the ruling class and those who were useful artisans were deported to Assyria and dispersed. Other nationalities were relocated to this region by Assyria, and, because of intermarrying, the Samaritans were no longer pure Israelites. In the eyes of the rest of Israel they had become an "inferior" race.

There were a group of Samaritans who, having been prevented from worshiping Yahweh in Jerusalem, withdrew to set up a place of worship of their own at Shechem. A temple was built on Mount Gerizim, and a distinctive faith gradually developed. The Samaritans accepted the five books of Moses as their authority, and this position was reflected in their creed: There is one God; Moses was his prophet and will one day be returning as the Taheb ("restorer," sometimes called "Messiah").

There was strong religious distrust between those who worshiped on Mount Gerizim and those who worshiped at the Temple in Jerusalem. In 128 B.C., one of the Jewish Hasmonean rulers (John Hyrcanus) captured Shechem and destroyed the temple. Somewhere between 6 and 9 A.D., a group of Samaritans defiled the Temple in Jerusalem by scattering bones there during Passover. The age-old resentment and distrust still remained at the time of Christ.

7. Although most Jews would not pass through Samaria, Jesus chooses to travel through the controversial province.

A. Why does Jesus choose this route? Consider both natural and spiritual reasons.

B. Samaria is mentioned by name in the following scriptures. What are the positive implications from these passages about Samaritans?

Luke 10:30-37

Acts 1:8

Acts 8:4-8, 14-17

8. In verse 14, the word for spring is *pege* meaning a fountain or spring. Welling up(*hallomai*) means to leap, spring, or bubble up.[36] Jesus promises a spring or well of living water bubbling up to eternal life, but the Samaritan woman is centered on the natural water from the well.

   A. How is Jacob's well different from the spiritual well of living water?

   B. What is Jesus actually offering to the Samaritan woman?

9. *God is Spirit* illustrates one of the four descriptions of God in the New Testament. The other three are *God is love*(1 John 4:8, 16), *God is light* (1 John 1:5), and *God is a consuming fire* (Hebrews 12:29).[37]

   A. What kind of worship is the Father seeking (verse 23-24)?

   B. What do you think it means to worship *in spirit and truth* (consider verses 21-22)?

10. As the revelation of his identity begins to unfold, Jesus boldly tells the Samaritan woman that he is the Messiah.

   A. What is her reaction (verse 28-30)?

   B. What is the result of her encounter with Christ (verses 39-42)?

11. The disciples return urging Jesus to eat something, but he is not hungry. He has been filled with a different type of food.

   A. What is the food that has satisfied Jesus (verse 32, 34)?

   B. In verses 35-38, Jesus draws an analogy between doing the will of God and the farmer's cycle of sowing and reaping. Identify and describe the following words with their evangelistic counterpart:

   Field:

   Harvest:

Sower:

Reaper:

C. According to Jesus, which is the hard work and which is the easy (verse 38)?

12. Who might be considered as modern-day Samaritans…those who have a measure of truth but have not experienced the fullness of being "born again?"

Woman Caught in Adultery
John 8:1-11

Jesus is once again in Jerusalem teaching in the temple courts. Hoping to discredit him among the people, a group of Pharisees and teachers of the law devise a test for him. They bring a woman caught in the act of adultery before the Master.

Under Mosaic Law, she should be condemned to death: *If a man commits adultery with another man's wife…both the adulterer and the adulteress must be put to death* (Leviticus 20:10). The penalty is defined by stoning both man and woman outside the gates of the city (Deuteronomy 22:22-24).

As these seemingly pious men drag and thrust the quivering woman before him, what will Jesus do? This was not an encounter with the Messiah that she chose and definitely not one that was joyfully anticipated. Would this Jesus condemn her according to the strict statutes of the Law of Moses or was there another way?

The Pharisees

The Pharisees were one of two religious parties prominent at the time of Christ. Their name means "those who separate themselves." There were around 6000 members of the association and their object was twofold: first, to observe in the strictest manner according to traditional law, all of the ordinances concerning Levitical purity. Second, they were extremely meticulous with religious dues and rituals. [38]

The Pharisees believed the Exile had been the cause of their ancestors breaking God's law. Consequently, they had a great zeal for remaining clean and obedient in the eyes of the law. The Pharisees believed in the historic doctrines of Judaism—in the unity, holiness and providence of God, the immortal soul bringing about a revival of the body, and in a final judgment and the election of Israel. The Pharisees survived all of the other groups and eventually became the founders of modern Judaism. [39]

13. Reflect on the woman's situation and her current surroundings. Also consider the Pharisees and teachers of the law who stand boldly in front of Jesus.

A. How would you describe her emotional and physical condition?

B. What does this incident relate about the heart condition of the Pharisees and teachers of the Law?

14. Jesus convicts the accusers with simple, yet indicting words. *If any of you is without sin, let him be the first to throw a stone at her* (John 8:7). In the end, no one is left to condemn the woman. The word for condemn is *katakrino* meaning to give judgment against, to judge worthy of punishment, to condemn, or by one's good example to render another's wickedness the more evident and censurable.[40]

A. Why can't the Pharisees and teachers of the law condemn her?

B. How does Jesus show her mercy?

C. What are Jesus' instructions to the woman (verse 11)?

Making it Personal

Through these close encounters with Christ, we have seen his truth and grace in amazing ways. Truth enlightened ignorance. Mercy triumphed over judgment. And nowhere did we see the harsh voice of an angry God condemning his wayward children.

Our mistakes, failures, and wrongdoings produce personal guilt and condemnation. Our reaction is usually to pull away from God because of inadequacy and shame. Adam experienced the same reaction—he hid from God after eating the forbidden fruit. But if you remember, God sought him out (Genesis 3). He was not limited by man's sin.

How well do you know your heavenly Father? Are you able to bask in his heavenly presence, resting in the assurance that he loves you? His desire is for you to know him intimately, confidant of his love. If you have struggled in this area, it may come as no surprise that your relationship with your earthly father is the filter by which you perceive your heavenly Father.

When I first came to the Lord at the age of twenty-nine, I was wounded in a number of areas that affected my perspective about my heavenly Father. I could relate to Jesus; I could understand the Holy Spirit, but I struggled with grasping the nature of a "Father." In his mercy, God extended his healing hand to me and began to mend my deep hurts. As he penetrated layer by layer with his gentle loving touch, I began to grasp the nature of a healthy relationship between a father and daughter as God intended. Month by month, year by year, he has revealed himself to me as Father in a way that I now appreciate, understand, and receive.

In the same way, Jesus is not restricted by our imperfections. He offers us truth that enlightens and sets us free. We need to view our Savior as the merciful, cleansing God that he is. There is no sin that is so vile that he cannot forgive. There is no transgression so monstrous that he cannot bridge the gulf. Guilt and condemnation from sin are meant to separate us from our God, but he has already made provision for our reconciliation.

As you reflect on these questions, open your heart to his inspection. Please don't reject the loving, compassionate relationship that is available to everyone. Allow God to enter into even the darkest closet of your past. He will cleanse and heal your every wound.

16. Read 1John 1:5-10.

   A. How can we walk in the truth (verse 7, 9)?

   B. According to verse 9, *If we_____ our sins, he is faithful and just and will _____ us our sins and _____ us from all unrighteousness.*

   C. What areas of your life need cleansing today? Pause, and apply the principles of 1 John 1:9 to your specific situations.

17. Jesus did not condemn the immorality of the women; instead he offered cleansing and forgiveness. As you examine the truth from the following scriptures, allow the Holy Spirit to remove any guilt and condemnation that still plagues you from past sins.

   Romans 8:1

   Ephesians 2:10

   Philippians 1:6

   Colossians 1:13-14

   Hebrews 4:14-16

   Father,

   I want to encounter and know you more intimately. There is nothing in my life that is hidden. You know my deepest thoughts and my innermost needs.

   I desire truth in my inner man, so I welcome your Spirit into these areas of my life. I realize I may have erected walls to surround my hurts and disappointments from the past. Please forgive me for pushing you away, for not trusting, and being unwilling to depend on you alone. Show me any hidden barriers, especially anyone who needs to be forgiven.

(Pause and allow the Holy Spirit to minister to you)

Forgive me, cleanse me, and restore me to fellowship with you. Break the burden of guilt, condemnation, and shame that have continued to haunt me. I thank you for your mercy extended to me. Thank you, Lord. You are the Light of my life who continually guides me along life's highway.

Amen

Notes

_____

_____

_____

_____

_____

_____

_____

_____

_____

Chapter Five
Seven Signs of the Messiah

*M*iracles and the technological age...can they coexist? Oh, yes! God is still in the miracle working business! I have seen his divine intervention in a powerful and compassionate way and can testify that He still remains on his throne. God is the same yesterday, today, and forever as attested to by the following story:

My robust, feisty grandmother Bubie was a highly independent lady. As the oldest sibling of nine brothers and sisters, she stood the tallest at five foot one! Whenever Bubie was around, we could guarantee that laughter, antics, and a bit of mischief would prevail. She would entertain us with song and dance as well as stories of her colorful youth as we sampled her latest culinary creation. We never knew exactly how old she was because she came through Ellis Island without a birth certificate!

When she was well into her nineties, I received news that Bubie had suddenly lapsed into a coma. She was taken to a local hospital and remained in that condition for over three days. The medical community said it was only a matter of time. Funeral preparations were underway.

Our family grieved over the impending loss—she was a one-of-a-kind individual. Over the years I had shared God's love with Bubie, sent her books on Yeshua, prayed with her, and for her. She always assured me that she knew God and prayed to him every morning. Yet, she had never received Jesus as her Savior.

On the afternoon of the third day, my husband and I were in her hospital room along with her two sisters, both well into their seventies. I was confused about what to do. I had prayed for her salvation for so many years, but what now?

With burdened hearts, we began to pray, and I released her into the hands of God. We asked God to take over and do whatever seemed best in his sight. To my amazement, within minutes Bubie awoke out of her coma. My two aunts were so excited they both started to exclaim, "It's a miracle, a miracle!"

Bubie turned to me and asked, "Am I dying?" I told her I didn't know, but what I did realize is that she needed to accept Yeshua as her Savior. That day in the hospital, my elderly Jewish grandmother prayed a prayer of repentance and received Jesus as her Savior.

God responds miraculously to the needs and prayers of his people. His miracles transcend the natural enter into the realm of the supernatural. I learned a lesson that day—nothing is impossible for our omnipotent God!

One of the distinguishing characteristics of The Gospel of John is the seven signs or miracles of Jesus. John judiciously selects seven such signs to validate Jesus as the Son of God, Israel's Messiah. All of the signs point to his Messianic nature. All demonstrate a special aspect of his supernatural power. All seven signs are unquestionably beyond the scope of human possibility.

The Greek word for sign is *semeion* and occurs 77 times in the New Testament. It translates as sign 50 times, miracle 23 times, wonder three times, and token once. A sign transcends the normal laws of nature. It is used throughout the New Testament as an indicator of divine activity.

The Pharisees and Sadducees demand a sign from Jesus to substantiate his claims(Matthew 12:38-3,Matthew 16:1-4); Herod expects Jesus to perform a miracle for him because he had heard of the miraculous accounts (Luke 23:8). Jesus himself stated, *Unless you people see signs and wonder…you will never believe.*(John 4:48)

John appeals to the current mindset of the people in his selection of the miracles. For example, there was Jewish expectation that the coming Messiah would put an end to hunger and thirst. Consequently, John highlights the feeding of the multitude and the miracle at Cana as Messianic proof. Nicodemus, a teacher of the law and familiar with Jewish tradition, recognizes that no one could do the signs Jesus does unless God is with him. As Jesus speaks what his Father speaks and does whatever he sees his Father do, he pulls heavenly reality into the earthly realm.

First Sign: Water to Wine
John 2:1-11

The first miraculous sign occurs within the backdrop of a Galilean wedding. The site of the wedding is the city of Cana in Galilee, the region surrounding the Sea of Galilee, and not far from Jesus' hometown of Nazareth.

A Jewish wedding is particularly significant to the community. They regard a wedding as an important event, almost a sacrament, with the most pious of Jews fasting and confessing sins before exchanging vows. To the Jew, the bridal pair on their wedding day symbolized the union of God and Israel. The event is a community celebration with everyone rising to greet the marriage procession or becoming a part of it. After the vows are exchanged, the wedding feast begins and could easily last more than one day.[41] It is this atmosphere that sets the stage for the first miraculous sign... changing water into wine.

The miracle of water into wine carries some prophetic implications. First, notice that Jesus' first miracle is at a wedding. Jesus himself would one day be wedded—to his bride the church. Second, the Jews believe purification comes from an outward cleansing with water, hence the water in the jars. However, Jesus will bring internal cleansing, a new wine of the spirit. Finally, the bridegroom is the one honored at this feast, not Jesus the source of the miracle. When the day arrives for the heavenly marriage of Jesus to his bride the church, Jesus the bridegroom will sit in the honored position.

The sign of turning water to wine also presents additional spiritual concepts to consider. This miracle emphasizes faith as a key component, the issue of timing during his ministry, and the disciple's resulting belief.

Water Jugs

The six stone jars were large water pots of about twenty gallons apiece. By the social rules of the day each guest was expected to ceremonially wash his hands before and after eating. In addition, water was used to ceremonially cleanse the vessels used; therefore, a considerable amount of water would be needed.

At least 120 gallons of water were available to the wedding party, and when turned into wine would supply two thousand, four ounce glasses. It was customary to dilute the wine with three parts of water to one of wine so there would have been enough wine to last for many days.[42]

1. A lack of provisions for the wedding feast would bring a lingering disgrace on the newly married couple. Mary, the mother of Jesus, entreats him to act in the couple's behalf. Mary's faith in her son is rewarded as Jesus tells the servants to fill the jars with water and bring some to the master of the banquet.

    A. What happens to the water?

    B. How does the master of the banquet respond to the newly served wine?

    C. Who receives the honor from the master of the banquet?

    D. Not only was the water turned to wine, but it was the best wine. What does this say about the nature of our Savior?

2. The Greek word for belief (*pisteuo*) means to think to be true, to be persuaded of, to credit, or place confidence in. Belief refers to the conviction and trust within a man.[43] This miracle of tuning the water into wine illustrates some universal principles as to how God moves through faith in behalf of his children. Note the role each person plays in the miracle. Describe the faith each displays:

    A. Jesus

    B. Mary

    C. Servants

    D. Master of the Banquet

    E. Disciples

F. Why is faith an important component to the Christian walk?

Second Sign: Healing of a Boy

John 4:46-54

A short time passes since the first miracle at Cana. Jesus travels to Jerusalem and returns with a measure of fame to the familiar Galilee region. He is welcomed by the Galileans for they have witnessed his power and authority at the Passover Feast in Jerusalem.

As Jesus revisits Cana, the site of his first recorded miracle, an officer's son lies sick and dying. The identity of the royal official of Capernaum is unknown, only that he serves Herod in some official capacity. Many scholars point to Chuza, the steward of Herod's household, because his wife Joanna supports Christ's ministry out of her personal funds (Luke 8:3). She may have followed Jesus out of profound gratefulness for the miracle performed in behalf of her son. In desperation, this official seeks the Prophet to plead the case of his son.

Capernaum

Capernaum was a city in or near the plain of Gennesaret, probably close to the Sea of Galilee, and served as a center of Jesus' activity during a large portion of his public ministry. It was apparently of some significance during the time of Christ. Capernaum had a customs station, for it was here that Matthew was called to be a disciple. It was also the base of a detachment of Roman soldiers.

Although Jesus grew up in Nazareth, the gospels refer to Capernaum as his home. Here he interfaced with Peter and his household, taught in the synagogue, healed and exorcised many of the people. In spite of this, Capernaum did not respond favorably toward Jesus as the Messiah. He rebuked the city for its unbelief stating, "it shall be more tolerable for Sodom in the day of judgment than for you"(Matthew 11:23-24).[44]

3. The royal official has traveled 20-25 miles from Capernaum to find Jesus. He was probably a Gentile and makes the decision to ask a Jewish teacher for help.

A. What do you think prompts the official to seek Jesus?

B. What does the royal official need Jesus to do?

C. The official "begged" Jesus. The verb for begged (*erotao*) is to ask or request. In this passage, it is in the imperfect tense. It means repeated or persistent action.[45] What does this reveal about the official's state of mind?

D. What is the result of the official's request? How does this miracle take place?

4. This man experiences a dramatic change of faith during his encounter with Jesus. His initial faith is based on rumor, but his final level of faith rests upon a miraculous demonstration of power. Match the following steps of faith with their corresponding actions in the story:

___The official seeks Jesus.

___Jesus promises the official healing. The man takes Jesus at his word.

___ Son is healed.

___The entire household believes.

A. Faith confirmed.

B. Faith based on hearsay…believing the rumors and reports.

C. Fruit of faith.

D. Faith ignited and active.

Third Sign: The Pool of Bethesda
John 5: 1-47

The site of this third sign is the Pool of Bethesda or "house of mercy" in Jerusalem. This pool of water is surrounded by five porches and located close to the sheep-gate and market. Under these porches or colonnades a large number of infirmed people wait expectantly for the *troubling of the water.*[46]

Jewish belief at this time attaches power and activity to angels. They believe special angels are localized in rivers and springs and offer miraculous cures.[47] A man with a long-term infirmity lays next to the pool hoping for such a cure. As Jesus passes by, his life is about to change dramatically.

Appealing first to his will, Jesus asks, *Do you want to get well?* This might seem like an unusual question…of course he wants to be well! But notice the excuses the invalid makes. *There is no one to help me. Someone else gets there first.* The long-term illness has affected more than just his physical body. Jesus is dealing not only with a physical infirmity, but with an emotional barrier that is preventing the healing from taking place. Nevertheless, after thirty-eight years of paralysis, the invalid picks up his mat and walks!

However, the Jewish authorities do not celebrate the miraculous healing. Instead, they confront

Jesus asking for an account of his misconduct. He has healed a man on the Sabbath, a day of rest and the invalid has carried his mat. Both are in violation of the Sabbath law.

Throughout the gospels, Jesus follows the Mosaic code and Jewish laws. He makes the pilgrimage to Jerusalem on the feast days, he teaches in the synagogue, observes Jewish ritual, and is called a Rabbi. Yet there are times when he openly infuriates the authorities. As Jesus comes into direct conflict here with the Jewish ruling powers, the area of controversy on this occasion is the fourth commandment *Remember the Sabbath day by keeping it holy* (Exodus 20:8-11).

The authorities are focused on the letter of the law—their hearts are hardened to the compassionate side of God's mercy. Is Jesus an unruly lawbreaker or does he answer to a higher source of justice?

Sabbath Law

As defined by Jewish law, the Sabbath began on Friday evening at sundown and lasted until Saturday evening at sundown. During this time all Jews were expected to observe the proper Sabbath rituals. They rested from their work and focused on God. However, the Sabbath Laws had become burdensome to the people. The Rabbis had added countless rules and regulations to the celebration of the Sabbath rendering the celebration a legalistic exercise.

Proper celebration of the Sabbath rested upon two principles...the avoidance of work and doing all which might make the Sabbath a delight. Fasting and mourning were prohibited. Food, dress, and every manner of enjoyment were prescribed in an attempt to make the Sabbath a joyous occasion.

In contrast, the innumerable regulations defining what work was, proved to be cumbersome. All work was arranged under thirty-nine chief classes, each of them having subordinate divisions. Therefore, "reaping" was a division and "plucking ears of corn" a lesser category underneath it. In addition, carrying an item was divided into two acts—picking it up and putting it down. A "burden" to be carried could be as small as a dried fig.

It became necessary to devise ingenious means to make ordinary life possible.[83] For example, a man was limited to travel only 2000 cubits (1 cubit=18 inches) on the Sabbath. However, if he left two meals at the boundary of that journey on Friday, it was then considered his dwelling and he could go on for another 2000 cubits.

It would break the Sabbath to climb a tree, ride, swim, clap one's hands, strike one's side or to dance. All judicial acts were prohibited on the Sabbath. This complicated code of external ordinances had transformed the holy Sabbath day prescribed by Moses into an endless exercise of legalistic behaviors.[48]

4. Even though a man is healed miraculously, the Jewish authorities struggle with aspects of the law.

    A. What two infractions of the law anger the Jewish authorities (verse 18)?

1.

2.

B. What is the result of their anger (verse 16)?

C. What does the Apostle Paul say about the law and the spirit in 2 Corinthians 3:6?

6. In verse 17 Jesus declares that his Father is *always working* and that he is *at work*. John's use of the term "work" refers to the deeds that reveal Jesus' divine nature.[49]

A. According to verses 19 and 30, what can the Son do by himself?

B. What has the Father given to the Son?

Verse 21, 26

Verse 22, 27

C. The ultimate purpose of the Father is (verse 23)_____.

7. The use of *akouo*, the Greek word for "hear," reflects the importance of God's Word as it is spoken and heard. True Biblical hearing involves receiving and responding to the call of repentance. This means that the only marks to distinguish true spiritual hearing from purely physical hearing are faith and action.[50] What three things does Jesus promise to those who hear his words (verse 24)?

A.

B.

C.

8. Jesus refers to two types of praise in verse 41-44. What are they? (The word for praise in this instance is the same word as glory.)

A.

B.

The Fourth Sign: Feeding the Multitude

John 6:1-4

Chapter 6 of the Gospel of John marks the height of Jesus' ministry and the turning point for the gospel. The masses are thronging to him hoping to witness a miracle at his hand. The offhand resistance from the Jewish religious authorities, scattered remarks, and opposition will now begin to fuse into a focused effort to destroy this renegade prophet.

The miracle of the fish and loaves, the fourth sign documented by John, occurs just before the Feast of Passover, a significant fact not to be overlooked. Passover is the feast that requires unleavened bread (leaven represents sin) to be eaten for seven days. In addition, it is quite possible that many of the five thousand that gathered on the slopes of Galilee were pilgrims traveling to Jerusalem to celebrate the feast. It is this backdrop that sets the stage for the fourth sign.

In addition, the disciples have recently returned from their first missionary journey. Sent out two-by-two, they travelled the countryside healing the sick and preaching the kingdom of God. Now, by the Sea of Galilee surrounded by the multitude of people, Jesus will further the education of his disciples.

As the people fill themselves with the bread and fishes, they are reminded of a scripture in Deuteronomy 18:15. Moses said God would *raise up a prophet like me from among your own brothers.* Like the Pharisees who ask John the Baptist whether he was the Prophet, these people question among themselves whether Jesus is the Prophet of whom Moses spoke. If he is the One, they are ready to make him king.

Barley and Wheat

The two main grains mentioned in Biblical accounts are barley and wheat. Barley formed the major part of the staple food of Palestine, particularly of the poorer classes. It had a shorter growing season than wheat. Therefore, it was harvested earlier in the growing season, and could flourish on poorer soil. Barley was also used as fodder for horses and cattle and for brewing, judging from evidence of Philistine drinking vessels.

Wheat formed an important part of the diet of the Israelites, and the wheat harvest was used as a Jewish calendar reference. Because of its importance as a food, it was a symbol of God's goodness and provision. It was used as a cereal offering in the Temple and formed part of the sacrifice made by David on Oman's threshing floor.[51]

9. The crowds sit and listen all day; night is drawing near and Jesus is concerned for the well-being of the people. He turns to his disciples who had just returned from their first missionary journey where they preached the gospel and healed multitudes of people. In John 6:6, Jesus

decides to "test" his disciples. The word for test (*peirazo*) means to try to learn the nature or character of someone or something by submitting such to thorough and extensive testing—to test, to examine, to put to the test.[52]

   A. With reference to Luke 9:12, what solution do the disciples recommend?

   B. What is Jesus' response in Luke 9:13?

   C. What is Philip's answer to the dilemma in John 6:7?

   D. What does Andrew suggest in John 6:8-9?

   E. How would you describe the faith of the twelve apostles at this time?

10. As a Jew, Jesus blesses the bread as the main staple of the meal with the traditional benediction, *Blessed art thou, Jehovah our God, King of the world, who causes to come forth bread from the earth.* What is the result of his prayer?

11. The notion of a coming Prophet is a popular expectation of this generation. Jesus, like Moses, has fed the multitude with supernatural provision.

   A. How do the people respond to this miracle of Jesus (verse 14-15)?

   B. This is the height of Jesus' popularity among the Jewish masses. He makes a crucial decision that sets the course for the rest of his ministry. How does Jesus respond to their ardent desire to make him an earthly king (verse 15)?

The Fifth Sign: Walking on Water
John 6:16-21

In the wake of the feeding of the multitude, Jesus now demonstrates his power and authority even over the natural elements of sea and sky. What a sight to behold…Jesus defying the laws of nature, calmly pressing through the stormy seas and bellowing winds to find his distraught disciples! In their haste, they had decided to row across the broad expanse of the Galilee without him. Bad decision!

12. The disciples embark on their voyage without Jesus. Consequently, there are two storms raging in this scenario—the storm of wind and rough waters and the storm in the hearts and minds of the disciples.

A. What is their response when they first see him walking on the water?

B. How does Jesus resolve both disturbances?

13. Matthew and Mark also include this miracle of Jesus in their respective gospels. What additional information do they choose to relate?

A. Matthew 14:25-33

B. Mark 6:45-52

The Sixth Sign: The Blind See
John 9:1-41

John Newton was a former slave trader who made his livelihood trafficking human flesh. He penned these words: *Amazing grace, how sweet the sound that saved a wretch like me. I once was lost, but now I'm found. Was blind, but now I see.* Jesus the Messiah, the Light of the World, brought light to his spiritual blindness!

The sixth sign of the gospel follows Jesus' proclamation in Chapter 8 that he is the *Light of the World.* It is almost a continuation of his statement…in essence an illustration of the truth of his words. Here he confronts blindness on two levels, physical blindness and spiritual blindness.

As he passes a blind man begging outside the temple, Jesus grasps the opportunity to graphically display his previous declaration of truth, *I AM the Light of the World.* Using his saliva, considered in Biblical times to have healing properties,he spits on the ground, makes some mud, and puts it in the man's eyes. After washing in the Pool of Siloam, the man blind from birth immediately receives his sight!

Controversy breaks out. Jesus breaks the Sabbath laws again, this time with two infractions. First, he heals a blind man on the Sabbath, and second he makes clay out of dirt and his spittle, an act of work prohibited on the Sabbath.

As the former blind man is brought before the Pharisees for questioning, they are openly divided about the miracle. Investigating further, they interrogate his parents, and dissatisfied with their explanation, the Pharisees summon the blind man once again.

The word for summon (*phoneo*) indicates they called, shouted for, cried out, spoke loudly, said with emphasis.[53] This was not a mere invitation, but an angry command to appear before them. As the Pharisees question the man, they make the statement *we know this man is a sinner*. The Greek text emphasizes the "we" and suggests that they are fully assured of their judgment.[54]

As the interrogation proceeds, the frustration of the Pharisees becomes apparent. The blind man
56

is not as docile as his parents. Instead, he confronts the biased arguments of the Pharisees. After every attempt to sway the man from his testimony, they finally explode and throw him out. Their spiritual darkness cannot overwhelm the spiritual light beaming from his eyes.

The blind man's faith has been increasing as evidenced by the sequence of titles used to describe Jesus. In verse 11, he refers to *the man they call Jesus*. In verse 17 he states that Jesus is a prophet. In verse 33 Jesus becomes the Son of Man. And in verse 38 he addresses Jesus as Lord. Finally, looking upon Jesus for the first time, the former blind man receives spiritual as well as natural sight.

Sin and Disease

During Biblical times, disease was a major problem. It included leprosy, diseases of diet and pollution (dysentery, cholera, typhoid, beri beri, dropsy), blindness, deafness, and crippling diseases. Epilepsy and other nervous disorders were also present.

Physicians were common in the community. Every town was required to have a physician and there was always a doctor in the Temple to look after the priests who had picked up things through their habit of walking barefoot.[55]

It was a common Jewish view that the merits and demerits of the parents would appear in the children. In fact, a child up to thirteen years of age was considered part of his father and suffered for his guilt. In addition, the thoughts of a mother might affect the moral state of her unborn offspring. Lastly, certain sins in the parents would result in specific diseases in their offspring, such as blindness.[56]

Jesus' regarded disease as the result of Satan's evil activity in the world, and as such it must be combated. However, Jesus did not believe that all disease was necessarily the result of individual sin. Some diseases were the result of spirit possession and he dealt with them accordingly.[57]

14. When the disciples look upon the blind man, they examine him through religious traditions and misconceptions. Exodus 34:7 states that God...*does not leave the guilty unpunished; he punishes the children and their children for the sin of the parents to the third and fourth generation.*

A. How do the disciples view the blind man's situation (verse 2)?

B. The Pharisees also refer to their traditional understanding of blindness. How do the Pharisees view the man (verse 33)?

C. How does Jesus see the man?

15. How do these four varied groups react to the miracle of the blind man's recovery of sight? How could this be a clue as to their spiritual condition?

Neighbors (verse 9,13):

Pharisees (verse 16):

Parents (verse 20-22):

Blind Man (verse 17):

16. The blind man begins to challenge the rationale of these Pharisees. As the tables turn, consider the boldness of the blind man. He is actually lecturing the learned Pharisees on religious doctrine.

    A. What is the reaction of the Pharisees (verse 28)?

    B. Who do the Pharisees believe they follow (verse 29)?

17. After hearing of his excommunication, Jesus takes the initiative and actively seeks the blind man to complete his journey of faith.

    A. The crucial element (verse 35, 36, 38) in the blind man's journey in faith is_____.

    B. What is the blind man's response to Jesus when he spiritually "sees" him for the first time?

18. According to verse 39, why does Jesus come into the world?

    A. Who are the blind ones?

    B. What is the condition of the blind (verse 41)?

Excommunication

The Talmud, a collection of ancient Jewish writings that makes up the basis of Jewish religious law, speaks of three types of excommunication. The first two were merely disciplinary while the third was the real "casting out" or cutting off from the congregation.

The first and lightest degree was the so-called Neziphah or a rebuke. Any three persons, or even one duly authorized, could pronounce this sentence. Ordinarily it lasted seven days, but if pronounced by the head of the Sanhedrin, it lasted thirty days.

The second degree of Jewish excommunication was the Niddui, which lasted thirty days. At the end of this period a second admonition was given lasting an additional thirty days. If one remained unrepentant, the real excommunication was pronounced and called the Cherem. Its length was indefinite and required an assembly of ten. The pronouncement was accompanied by curses and sometimes a blast of a horn.

The results of excommunication were costly. The person was treated as being dead. He was not allowed to study with others, communication was forbidden, he was not even to be shown the road. He might buy the necessities of life, but it was unlawful to eat or drink with him.[58] This constant threat of excommunication loomed over the heads of the people.

The Seventh Sign: The Dead Raised

John 11:1-57

The seventh and final sign is the climax of Jesus' miracles is unique to the Gospel of John. It depicts Jesus exhibiting the ultimate supernatural display of power and authority…raising his friend Lazarus from the dead. Jesus proclaims himself *the resurrection and the life* and then demonstrates his ability to conquer even the final adversary of death.

Jesus' arrival in Bethany occurs four days after the death of Lazarus. According to Jewish custom, Lazarus is buried on the day of his death. He has been dead for four days. The Jews believe that on the fourth day following death, the soul, which has lingered near the body, finally departs and bodily corruption sets in.[59]The fact that this sign occurs on the fourth day indicates that Lazarus is truly dead, and as Mary states in verse 39, *there is a bad odor.*

It is customary for mourners to gather around the family and mourn for days, and so "many Jews had come to comfort them." The family is probably well known in Jerusalem where many of the mourners live and they have connections to the Jewish leaders.[60] This is the pervading atmosphere that greets Jesus as he meets Martha and Mary in the road.

In this confrontation with death itself, we see the godly compassion of our Lord as well as his "human" emotions. *He wept* is the shortest verse in the Bible. It is found in John 11:35 and speaks to us of Jesus' humanity. He is touched with our weaknesses and earthly struggles.

Lazarus is not buried in a cemetery. Instead, he is placed in his own private tomb in a cave, probably surrounded by a garden, the favorite place of interment. Not only the rich, but also the moderately well-to-do had tombs of their own which were acquired and prepared long before needed. Their bodies would be anointed with spices, myrtle, aloe, hyssop, rose oil, and rose water. The body dressed and wrapped in cloths in which a Roll of the Law would be laid. Lazarus is left in this condition until the call to come out.[61] Awakened by the authoritative voice of his Lord, Lazarus walks out of the tomb!

The raising of Lazarus becomes the final event that spurs the Jewish authorities into action. In a desperate move to retain their power and status in the land, the Sanhedrin decides *one man should die for the nation.* Everything they hope to gain (power, autonomy, control) will eventually be lost because of their blind religious dogma and ambition.

The Mourners

One of the most binding of Rabbinic directives was to comfort the family who had lost a loved one. The official period of mourning began before the burial, shared by friends who sat silent on the ground, or were busy preparing the mourning meal.

The funeral procession followed, men and women separated, with the women returning alone from the gravesite. The funeral oration would be delivered and the dead was supposed to be present listening to the words of the speaker and watching the expressions on the faces of the hearers. As the company left the dead, each would say" Depart in peace." They then formed lines through which the mourners passed amidst expressions of sympathy echoed at least seven times.

The real mourning began in the house and would last thirty days, of which the first three were the greatest. The dead would be spoken of and biblical passages applied to their memory. Whenever they were mentioned again, a blessing would be added to their memory. On the Sabbath the mourners rested in accordance with the commandments.[62]

19. While in Perea, Jesus receives a distressful message from Mary and Martha, two sisters, who live in Bethany. Jesus responds to the message in an uncharacteristic manner. Instead of rushing off immediately to aid Lazarus, he waits two additional days before returning to Bethany.

A. Why were the sisters distressed (verse 3)?

B. According to Jesus, what purpose will Lazarus' illness serve (verse 4, 15)?

C. How do the disciples respond to his return to Jerusalem (verse 8, 16)?

20. As Jesus and Martha begin their discussion, Martha exhibits a faith in the Master based on previous encounters. She trusts Jesus as her Lord, and, accordingly, lays the foundation for a wondrous move of God.

A. In verse 21, what two specific beliefs does Martha state?

1.

2.

B. Martha believes Lazarus will rise again in the last days. What does she refer to?

C. Jesus expands Martha's thinking in verse 25 by declaring the he is *the resurrection and the life*. He uses a key word three times in verse 25-26. What is the key to this impending miracle?

D. Responding boldly and with great conviction, Martha answers with a revelatory description echoing Peter's declaration of Jesus as the Christ (Matthew16:16). What are the four descriptive names that Martha uses for Jesus?

1.

2.

3.

4. (verse 28)

21. As a preamble to this miracle of resurrection, Jesus prays to the Father in verse 41-42. The summons for Lazarus to come forth is reminiscent of Jesus words in John 5:28, when a time will come when *all who are in their graves will hear the voice of the Lord and come out*.

A. Where does Jesus place his confidence?

B. Why does Jesus pray openly in front of this crowd of mourners?

C. In this last sign, what part do the onlookers play (verse 39, 44)?

D. What similarities do you see between the raising of Lazarus and the spiritual rebirth of a new believer?

22. The Jewish religious hierarchy is decidedly against Jesus. The time for the Passover draws

near. The authorities reach the point of no return. The stage is set for the final days of Jesus' ministry.

A. What threatened the Jewish authorities (verse 48)?

B. What is the outcome of the Sanhedrin's meeting (verse 53,54,57)?

Sanhedrin

Jewish law and order were organized into three tribunals. In towns numbering less than 120 males, three judges were appointed to oversee the lowest level of jurisdiction. The second level consisted of twenty-three men, also limited in their jurisdiction. Both were appointed by the Great Sanhedrin in Jerusalem.

The Great Sanhedrin consisted of seventy-one members, and appointment to it came from the tribunal itself. Either one of the lower tribunals would be promoted, or one in the first three rows of disciples who sat facing the judges was chosen.

It was presided over by the Nasi or president of the Sanhedrin. At least twenty-three members were required for a quorum and the judges sat in a semicircle.

Students were allowed to speak in favor of an accused, but not against him. Two writers recorded both the favorable and unfavorable remarks. The voting began with the youngest going first, so that the elders would not influence the juniors.

The Great Sanhedrin administered justice, especially in all religious areas and inferior areas of judgment. Because the High Priest was an appointment of Herod and the Procurators of Rome, in great criminal cases the High Priest would preside over the Sanhedrin instead of the "Nasi." Herod always reserved the right of final disposition in all cases. [63]

Making It Personal

The seven signs of Christ spoke to the people of Israel in the first century, but they also communicate to us today. Their message challenges us to think beyond the natural and embrace the supernatural power of a living Savior.

The Apostle Paul records in Corinthians that we only "know in part." Much like the disciples, Jesus renews and transforms our minds so that we, too, can walk in the fullness of his light. As God continues to reveal new and deeper truths through his word, he compels us to embrace them.

Faith is also a prominent component in these signs and an integral part of the Christian walk. James 1:2-4 simply states that the *testing of our faith develops perseverance...so that we may be mature and complete not lacking anything*. In the miracle of raising Lazarus from the dead, Jesus chose two sisters who knew him and loved him. He challenged them to believe for the miraculous.

Was Martha and Mary's faith tried—yes, indeed! Was the outcome beyond anything they could have imagined or hoped for? Without a doubt, yes. And did they mature and become more complete in the process? Certainly, their testimony of Christ became unshakable. As God perfects our faith, what seems to be trying and overwhelming, is only a rung in the ladder of maturity.

Is there a situation paralyzing you at your own Pool of Bethesda? Has your dream died? Do you need a touch today from the Healer?

We serve a wonderful and powerful Savior who is still able to challenge natural forces, heal the sick, and even raise the dead. Our merciful, dynamic Jesus still performs miracles!

As we take time to reflect on the nature of our risen Saviour, remember he is the same today as he was two thousand years ago. What holds you back from receiving his powerful touch?

23.The invalid had a preconceived notion of how he would be healed, but his ideas limited the hand of God. Human traditions, preconceived ideas, false religious doctrine, and a lack of faith can hinder the power of God.

A. How might you be limiting the hand of God from moving in your situation?

B. How could you remove any obstacle preventing your breakthrough?

C. Are you willing to be unconventional to receive God's best in your life?

24. Medical science has proven unhealthy emotions are the root cause of most physical illness. When the past still afflicts our mind, will and emotions, our wounded souls become an open door for disease and ill health.

A. Take an honest inventory of your soul. What areas or situations are still festering within?

B. The following scriptures shed some light on some underlying reasons for many problems we face:

1 Samuel 15:23

Matthew 7:1-5

Matthew 18:23-25

Ephesians 4:26

Ephesians 4:31

25. Hebrews 2:3-4 states: *This salvation, which was first announced by the Lord, was confirmed to us by those who heard him. God also testified to it by signs, wonders and various miracles, and by gifts of the Holy Spirit distributed according to his will.* How does God use signs to continue the work of the gospel?

Dear God,

Thank you for your faithfulness to me. Without your steady hand to guide me and your grace to uphold me, I would be lost and without hope. I thank you that you love me, that you will never leave or forsake me. Your love is a constant through all of my victories and all of my struggles.

Help my faith to grow and mature as I walk daily with you. Please uproot the lies that have bound me, and release me into a new realm of truth and freedom.

I BELIEVE that your power is available to me today. All authority belongs to you.

I RECEIVE your power to heal, transform, and bring new life to any and all dead areas of my life. (pause and allow the Holy Spirit to minister to you)

Lord, I give you the freedom to move in whatever way seems best to you.

Thank you for hearing my prayer and loving me. You are a mighty God!

Amen

Notes

Chapter Six

I AM

Another significant characteristic of the Gospel of John is the seven "I AM's" of Christ. By using these expressions, Jesus makes an unmistakable claim to be YHWH (Yahweh), the God of Israel.

The seven I AM's are rooted in the Old Testament book of Exodus. God appears to Moses and asks him to return to Egypt and lead the Israelites to freedom. Moses responds with a question, *"Suppose I go to the Israelites and say to them, 'The God of your fathers has sent me to you,' and they ask me, 'What is his name?'"* (Exodus 3:13) God announces his name to Moses stating,

> *God said to Moses, I AM WHO I AM. This is what you are to say to the Israelites: I AM has sent me to you.*
>
> *God also said to Moses, Say to the Israelites, 'The LORD, the God of your fathers— the God of Abraham, the God of Isaac and the God of Jacob—has sent me to you.' This is my name forever, the name you shall call me from generation to generation. (Exodus 3:14-15)*

Jahweh…Jehovah

I AM is a form of the Hebrew word "to be," a personalized name for Yahweh, expressed as "LORD" in the Bible. When Jesus speaks these words, he expresses it as the Greek *ego eimi*, which stresses the first words as I AM. For Jesus to refer to himself as I AM is an unmistakable claim to be God himself.[64]

> *"Very truly I tell you," Jesus answered, "before Abraham was born, I am!" John 8:58 (NIV)*

Each of the vivid statements proclaims his deity and presents a picture of Christ as the fulfillment of scripture. Each saying holds meaning for the people of that time, embodies a particular facet of Christ's nature, and provides a revelation of how humanity can relate to the divine. Through these seven statements, Jesus leaves no doubt that he is who he claims to be.

I Am the Bread of Life

John 6:22-70

This first I AM follows the miracle of the fish and loaves which ties into the Jewish expectations of the Messiah. They anticipate a fabulous Messianic banquet surrounded by fruit trees that yield every day, grain harvests without reaping or winnowing, and ordinary trees that produce like fruit trees. Every imaginable type of produce will be found in Palestine in abundance and luxury when the Messiah finally arrives![65] Food will be supernaturally provided similar to the manna in the wilderness fifteen hundred years before.

The miracle of the loaves and fishes feeds this fantasy. A tradition among the Jews states, "as the first Redeemer caused manna to fall from heaven, even so should the second Redeemer cause the manna to fall."[66] The Jews look to Jesus as this future provider of their physical food.

Redirecting the multitude's carnal thoughts about bread to the spiritual truths about himself, Jesus announces *I AM the Bread of Life* (John 6:35). He does this by drawing upon the people's familiar knowledge of bread in their culture. First, bread is a staple of their diet and the essence of their existence. To first century Israel, bread is a vital element of life. Second, bread holds spiritual significance to Israel. The showbread in the Temple and the meal offerings upon the altar both speak prophetically of the coming Messiah. Jesus is both—the daily sustenance that they need to live and the promised Messiah. Manna and the bread of heaven come down from the Father

Instead of a joyous reception at this revelation, the crowd reacts much like Israel of old...they murmur, doubt, and complain. Their rational minds take over and they begin to reject the spiritual truths that Jesus had just presented.

As Jesus instructs the crowds, he states that they must *eat his flesh and drink his blood.* To the natural Jewish mindset, this borders on gross sin. The Law of Moses forbids any drinking of blood under penalty of being cut off from the people.[67] Because they fail to grasp the spiritual implications, many depart from Jesus, leaving only the twelve disciples.

This portion of the discourse occurs in the synagogue in Capernaum. Among the modern-day ruins of this place of worship, a lintel bears the insignia of a pot of manna ornamented with a flowing pattern of vine leaves and clusters of grapes.[68] These were the outward emblems of the Lord's teaching on that day.

Bread

Bread was so basic a food that it became synonymous with life itself. "Eating bread" was the equivalent phrase for "having a meal." "Give us each day our daily bread" was a prayer for daily provision of food itself. [69]

Kneading in wooden bowls or kneading troughs prepared dough. It was mixed with leaven and made into thin cakes, round or oval, and then baked. In the towns, there were public ovens and bakers by trade whose ovens were not unlike those of modern times.

The shew-bread, or bread of the presence, consisted of twelve loaves of unleavened bread prepared and presented hot on the golden table in the Temple every Sabbath. They were square or oblong, and represented the twelve tribes of Israel. The old loaves were removed every Sabbath, and were to be eaten only by the priests in the court of the sanctuary.[70]

1. Jesus perceives the unspiritual motives of the multitude that follow him. They have been fed with the loaves and fishes and now want more.

    A. In verse 26, why are the people searching for Jesus?

    B. What type of food is Jesus really offering to them (verse 27)?

2. Jesus corrects their theology in respect to Moses. They believed that although God had given them the bread, it had come through the merits of Moses and ceased with his death.[71]

    A. What are the two types of bread (verse 31-32)?

    B. Who gives the *true bread* from heaven (verse 32)?

    C. What is this *true bread* and what does it provide (verse 33)?

    D. In answer to their request for the *true bread* from heaven, Jesus boldly states, *I AM the Bread of Life*. What does he promise the people that receive him(verse 35)?

3. Jesus has come from heaven as the *true bread* to do the will of the Father. Specifically, what does Jesus state in this passage as the Father's will (verses 39-40)?

    A.

    B.

    C.

4. The words *eat my flesh and drink my blood* cause many to pull back from Jesus. These words have also caused division throughout the history of the church universal. In regards to the "flesh and the blood" being elements of communion, the Roman Catholic Church points to this verse as the basis for their belief in transubstantiation (the elements of bread and wine actually changed into the body and blood of Christ). The Lutheran view of consubstantiation (Jesus' body and blood present in the elements, but not literally the body and blood of Christ) also stem from this verse.[72] Some see this statement as being a "spiritual" representation and the elements as symbolic. Others believe they are a memorial for Jesus' body and blood.

    A. According to each verse, what does "eating Jesus' flesh and drinking his blood" provide?

      Verse 53

      Verse 54

      Verse 56

B. How do you view the elements of communion in respect to Jesus' flesh and blood?

5. Consider the fact that among these people, some may have been Sadducees, another political party in the religious hierarchy. The Sadducees did not believe in the resurrection, yet Jesus speaks of "raising them up in the last days" four different times (verse 39, 40, 44, 54). How would this have influenced their decision to reject Jesus?

6. Jesus addresses his disciples and asks if they are offended? The word is *skandalon*, to put a stumbling block or impediment in the way upon which another may trip and fall, to distrust and desert one whom he ought to trust and obey.[73] Their skepticism was expressed in their grumbling. The hard saying of Jesus about eating and drinking his flesh and blood brings them to a juncture.

    A. In verse 63, what does Jesus state about the words he has spoken?

    B. What response does he receive from many of his disciples (verse 66)?

    C. Peter, speaking for the Twelve, gives what affirmative response (verse 68)?

I Am the Light of the World

John 8:12-59

The second I AM proclamation of Jesus immediately follows the Feast of Tabernacles in Chapter Seven, possibly the next day. Jesus is again teaching in the temple, this time *near the place where the offerings are put.*

The treasury is located in the Court of the Women, the common meeting place of worshipers and the most attended part of the Temple. The Court of the Women obtained its name, not from the exclusive use of women, but because they were not allowed to proceed farther except for sacrificial purposes. The court covered a space of about 200 square feet. Around it ran a simple colonnade and within it, against the wall, were the thirteen chests for charitable contributions that were shaped like trumpets. Nine were for receipt of what was due from the worshipers; the other four were for voluntary gifts.[74]

On every night of the previous festival week, the darkness was brilliantly illuminated by a large Menorah (candlestick). In addition, wicks on tall torches shone brightly in the courtyard and cast their light across Jerusalem.[75] This was called "the joy of the feast."

The Jews believe God would kindle the "Great Light" and the nations of the world would point to them when the Messiah came. They assumed God was hiding the light under his throne and then it would shine forth once more.[76] Now at the close of the feast, the large Menorah remains lit in the Temple.

Light is a familiar theme throughout the Gospel of John. In the prologue, Jesus was the *light shining in darkness* which *the darkness could not understand or overwhelm*. The symbolic nature of Jesus as the light culminates here in Jesus' declaration, *I AM the light of the world*. As the brilliant light of God shines, truth becomes a beacon to liberate people from the bondage of sin and its affects. In the midst of the revelry, with torches and Menorahs blazing into the sky, Jesus points to himself as the fulfillment of their Messianic hopes.

The conversation between Jesus and the Pharisees continues as the question of Jesus' origin surfaces again. As Jesus explains where he came from, he cautions them as to their eternal state. Two prevalent phrases appear in this segment—"you will die in your sins" and "I am." Unfortunately, the Pharisees cannot grasp the revelation of truth that Jesus is presenting.

Jesus words and miracles have convinced a portion of the crowd, but their faith is based on tangible evidence, not in the person of Jesus. This group has a measure of faith, but it is lacking in real substance, and their reaction is, for the most part, a fleshly response to the supernatural.

When Jesus' words contradict the traditional patterns of thought, their weak foundation of faith crumbles easily. Genuine faith is required to be a disciple of Jesus, a faith that is based on truth.

As the conversation continues, Jesus is charged with being demon-possessed. This is the second of three times in the gospel (7:20, 8:52, 10:20) when the crowd accuses the Son of God. To be demon-possessed in this culture was equivalent to being mentally deranged or impaired. They still claim innocence based on their ancestral relationship to Abraham, but a greater one than Abraham confronts them.

Menorah

The Menorah was an object that supported one or more oil lamps. Although such stands could be made of stone, pottery, or wood, the biblical passages with one exception, describe golden lampstands.

Four successive lampstand traditions can be identified. First, Exodus describes a single golden lampstand composed of a central, cylindrical stand with three pairs of branches and elaborate floral decorations. Second, ten golden lampstands stood in Solomon's Temple. Third, the rebuilt Temple of the late sixth century, evidently resumed the single lampstand tradition. Fourth, the apocalyptic vision in the book of Revelation expands the single golden lampstand to seven.[77]

During the Feast of Tabernacles, four golden candelabras were used in Herod's Temple each with four golden bowls. Against them rested four ladders that youths of priestly descent climbed in order to fill each bowl with oil. The light from the Temple lit every court in Jerusalem.[78]

7. Jesus declares himself to be the "Light of the World." What two promises does Jesus make to his followers in verse 12?

A.

B.

8. Another constant theme in this portion of scripture is Jesus' reference to the Father. The underlying reason for the conflict with the Pharisees results from the fact that they don't really know him (verse 19). How does the Father support Jesus in each of these verses?

Verse 16

Verse 18

Verse 26

Verse 28

Verse 29

9. Jesus addresses the Jewish believers who are in the crowd with, *If you hold to my teaching…* This is the first usage of the word hold and is translated in other verses as abide. One of the undeniable proofs that Jesus exists is his ability to liberate our lives from sin and death. *Eleutheria* is the Greek word for "freedom from sin, the law, and death" and is used in verses 32 and 36. It is freedom from an existence in sin that leads to death.[79] It also carries the idea "to cause someone to be set free or to be released, to set free, to release."[80]

A. In verse 32, Jesus states that they will come to know the truth. What is the consequence of coming to know truth?

B. According to verse 36, how definitive is Jesus' liberating power?

C. The word *eleutheria* is also used in the following scriptures. Record the truths described in these passages.

Romans 8:2

Galatians 5:1

D. How does this truth apply to our lives?

10. Paternity is a constant issue. Jesus accuses the people of having a different father than God and this is the main reason for their spiritual blindness. Although Jesus has come to give them light, they choose to remain in their darkness.

   A. Who is their father?

   B. What are some of his characteristics (verse 44)?

   C. What is the primary reason the people will not listen to Jesus and receive his words (verse 47)?

Abraham

Abraham was a descendant of Shem and son of Terah; husband of Sarah and father of Isaac, ancestor of the Hebrew nation and, through Ishmael, of other Semites. Jew, Christian and Muslim consider his life recorded in Genesis to be an example of outstanding faith in God.

Israel was considered "the seed of Abraham," and Yahweh's action in raising a people from one man was held to be a particularly significant fulfillment of his word. The God of Abraham, designated Yahweh throughout Scripture, was the name whereby he revealed himself to Moses. Abraham's monotheism amidst idolatry, the way God appeared to him, chose, redeemed and blessed him, and Abraham's faith were a constant theme of exhortation and discussion.

In New Testament times, Abraham was revered as the ancestor of Israel, of the Levitical priesthood, and of the Messiah himself. Popular Jewish superstition thought that racial descent from Abraham brought divine blessings. His children inherited the oath, covenant, promise and blessing granted Abraham by God. Abraham's obedience by faith to his call from Ur to the nomadic life of a stranger and pilgrim and his offering of Isaac are listed as outstanding examples of faith in action.[81]

I Am the Gate; I Am the Good Shepherd

John 10:1-42

In one of the most beloved of all of the Psalms, David writes, *The Lord is my Shepherd* (Psalm 23). What insight David must have had into the joys, discipline, and hardships of being a shepherd. From the wealth of his shepherding experience, David metaphorically ascribes those same characteristics to God himself. The Lord *makes me lie down in green pastures* in order to feed the human soul with healthy sustenance. He *leads me beside quiet waters* to bring a time of refreshing and to quench spiritual thirst. *He guides me along the right paths* for that is the only path that the Shepherd knows. His *rod and staff comfort me* by bringing both protection and authority over those that are his.

The LORD is my shepherd, I lack nothing. He makes me lie down in green pastures, he leads me beside quiet waters, he refreshes my soul. He guides me along the right paths for his name's sake. Even though I walk through the darkest valley, I will fear no evil, for you are with me; your rod and your staff, they comfort me. You prepare a table before me in the presence of my enemies. You anoint my head with oil; my cup overflows. Surely your goodness and love will follow me all the days of my life, and I will dwell in the house of the LORD forever. Psalm 23:1–6 (NIV)

In the opening lines of Chapter Ten, Jesus distinguishes between the true shepherd and the thieves, those who enter the sheep pen by means other than the gate. At the entrance to the sheepfold, the gate is a low, arched building with a stone wall enclosure attached. A watchman stands guard over the flock securing them from thieves and robbers who might climb over the wall, slaughter the defenseless sheep, and throw them out to accomplices.[82]Jesus declaration of *I AM the gate for the sheep* establishes him as the one way, the entry point, and protector of God's divine flock.

The true shepherd of the Mideast cares for his sheep. During the day, the shepherd leads the sheep into the green hillsides for sustenance. At night, he encloses the sheep in a pen for their protection and lies down across the gate so that no intruder passes through.

The primary responsibilities of a biblical shepherd are 1) to watch for enemies trying to attack the sheep; 2) to defend the sheep from attackers; 3) to heal the wounded and sick sheep; 4) to find and save lost or trapped sheep; 5) to love them.[83] It is common for several herds of sheep to share the same sheepfold. In the morning, when the gate is opened, each shepherd picks out his own flock and each member of that flock is able to distinguish "his" shepherd from the others. The sheep know their shepherd's voice, just as God's people recognize Jesus as the living Word of God.[84]

By declaring *I AM the good shepherd*, Jesus sets himself apart from other shepherds in two distinctive ways. First, to announce he is a "good shepherd" indicates there have been "bad shepherds." Others have gone before him, and even stand before him now, as false prophets, false Messiahs, and artificial leaders over Israel that have brought harm to God's people. Second, his proclamation binds him unequivocally to the divine Yahweh, the Shepherd of Israel.

In the decades before Jesus' incarnation, numerous false prophets and Messiahs deceive the people and lead them astray. These false shepherds, persuasive zealots, and outright con men drew the masses into their snare. In contrast to Jesus the good shepherd, they were thieves and robbers who destroyed and plundered the heavenly flock.

In the second half of the chapter (verses 22-42), Jesus addresses the nature of the shepherd and sheep again during the Festival of Dedication. As these men confront the Good Shepherd, Jesus places the burden of belief back upon them. They interpret his statement "I and the Father are one" as blasphemous and are ready to fulfill their "legal" responsibility to stone Jesus. With an appeal to the picturesque example of God the Shepherd, Jesus openly beckons his sheep once more to hear his voice. This is Jesus' last regular visit to the Temple. His next appearance in Jerusalem will be during Passover at the time of his Passion.

Sheep

Sheep are mentioned in the Bible more than five hundred times. While most of the references in the Old Testament are literal, practically all references in the New Testament are metaphors comparing the relationship of Christ and his followers to that of the shepherd and his flock.

Sheep preferred flat or gently rolling grazing grounds and ate plants down to the root, thriving on the stubble left over from the barley and wheat harvest. The Bible provides several references to the skill of the shepherd, who knew each of his animals by name, whose voice was recognized by his sheep, and who took care of them in illness.

The constant search for greener pastures was a regular task for those who tended sheep. The importance of finding adequate shelter for the night sometimes led to the use of natural caves.

Sheep provided most necessities of life: milk, meat, hides, and wool. Even their horns were used as containers for oil or as musical instruments. The skins were usually made into clothing and the inner covering of the tabernacle was made from skins that had been dyed red.

Throughout the New Testament the sheep were used in a figurative sense for human beings. Jesus compared Israel to sheep lost and without a shepherd. Sheep also played a role in several parables of Jesus and the Gospel of John pictures Jesus as a protecting shepherd, willing to give his life for his sheep. The people whom Jesus fed he compared to sheep without a shepherd. He is himself compared to a sheep led to slaughter.[85]

11. The opening verses of this chapter are a *paroimia*, a symbolic or figurative saying; a speech or discourse in which a thing is illustrated by the use of similes and comparisons.[86] Jesus uses recognizable figures in the rural community like the shepherd, thieves, sheep, and gatekeeper. In verse seven, he unveils himself in this pastoral description with *I AM the gate for the sheep.* List the distinct qualities of each.

    A. Shepherd

        Verse 2

        Verse 3

        Verse 3

        Verse 4

Verse 11

B. Gatekeeper (Verse 3)

C. Thief (*kleptes*, "to steal, secretly and craftily to embezzle and appropriate,[87] the name is transferred to false teachers, who do not care to instruct men but abuse their confidence for their own gain)[88]

Robbers (*lestes*, those who try to bring in the kingdom without regard for Jesus, and who bring the flock into serious danger.[89] From a root meaning to win, to seize, come words for prey, and to seize as prey, and one who seizes prey)[90]

Verse 1

Verse 8

Verse 10

E. Sheep

Verse 3

Verse 4

Verse 5

Verse 9

Verse 9

F. The Gate (verse 9)

12. Verse 10 describes a sharp difference between Jesus and the thieves and robbers. They have come to steal (*klepto*, to commit a theft, take away by stealth[91]), kill (*thuo*, to sacrifice, immolate, to slay, kill, slaughter[92]), and destroy (*apollumi*, to put out of the way entirely, abolish, put an end to ruin, render useless, to perish, to be lost, ruined, destroyed[93]). Jesus comes to give people life (*zoe*, the absolute fullness of life, both essential and ethical, which belongs to God, life real and genuine, a life active and vigorous, devoted to God, blessed[94]), and that life to be full (*perissos*, over and above, more than is necessary, exceeding abundantly, superior,

extraordinary, surpassing, uncommon[95]).

A. Who are the thieves and robbers?

B. Describe some of the ways Jesus gives life, and its fullness.

13. The phrase *lay down my life* is exclusive to John's writings and signifies a voluntary sacrificial act. Life (*psyche*) is more than physical existence; it involves personality and is more frequently translated as soul. Jesus as the Good Shepherd stands ready to sacrifice his total self for the sake of his sheep.[96]

A. How does Jesus "lay down his life?" (Consider his present role and his future)

B. What command and authority did Jesus receive from his Father (verse 18)?

14. In verse 16, Jesus mentions sheep that are not of "this sheep pen." With reference to Ephesians 2:11-16, who is he describing?

The Feast of Dedication

Better known today as Hanukkah, the Feast of Dedication commemorates the purification of the Temple in the time of the Maccabean revolt. On the 25th of Kislev (December), 167 B.C., during the religious persecution of the Jews by the Seleucid Antiochus Epiphanes, the altar of the Temple was polluted with pagan sacrifices. Observant Jews, under the leadership of Mattathias (a priest) and his five sons, rebelled against the Seleucids. Upon Mattathias' death, his son Judas Maccabee took command of the revolt, won several victories over the Seleucid army, and reconquered Jerusalem.

After cleansing the Temple, rebuilding the sanctuary, consecrating the courts, and making a new sacrificial altar with holy vessels, they burned incense on the altar and lit the lamps on the lampstand. A legendary story exists of a small cruse of holy oil discovered at the cleansing of the Temple that was miraculously able to light the Temple lamp for eight days until more oil could be supplied.

Judas and the people determined that the days of dedication should be celebrated annually beginning with the 25th of Kislev and lasting for eight days. Hanukkah thus became the only Jewish festival not ordained in the Hebrew Bible.[97]

15. Verses 28 and 29 utilize two vibrant words from the Greek language—perish, (*apollumi*, to destroy, to put out of the way entirely, abolish, put an end to ruin, render useless[98]) and snatch (*harpazo*, to seize, carry off by force.)[99]

A. What eternal assurance do the true sheep have (verses 28-29)?

B. What statement does Jesus make which underscores this assurance?

I Am the Resurrection and the Life

John 11:25

The fifth I AM statement occurs in the midst of the Lazarus account studied in Lesson 5. Jesus declares to Martha *I AM the resurrection and the life*.

The concept of resurrection is not new to the Jews; however, the idea is controversial and divides the two religious parties of Pharisees and Sadducees. The Sadducees do not believe in a resurrection. The Pharisees, in contrast, adhere to this spiritual expectation as part of God's eternal plan.

As a large portion of Judaism believes in a resurrection, Jesus becomes the vessel through which their resurrection is accessible. It is through Jesus that Lazarus is raised, and only through him that believers experience a rebirth into eternal life.

Sadducees

Their name was derived from saddiq (righteous) and from the name Zadok (either the high priest or another). They were primarily a religious group of priestly conservatives, the Judaean aristocracy through a supposed link with the priesthood, and a political party.

The religious dogma of the Sadducees denied divine action in the world, affirmed human freedom, and believed that the soul perishes along with the body. The Sadducees rejected beliefs in the afterlife, resurrection and a postmortem judgment. They had the support of the rich and accepted only the written laws in contrast to the Pharisee's traditions.[138]

There were many Sadducees among the "elders" of the Sanhedrin. They seem, indeed, to have been as numerous as the Pharisees and showed their hatred of Jesus in taking part in his condemnation. They endeavored to prohibit the apostles from preaching the resurrection of Christ and were the deists or skeptics of that age. They do not appear as a separate sect after the destruction of Jerusalem in 70 A.D.[100]

16. The word resurrection, *anastasis*, means to raise from a lower status to a higher one.[101] For Christians this relates to the promise of a new life with a new resurrected body in eternity.

A. What does Jesus imply to Martha with his bold statement *I AM the resurrection and the life*?

B. The theme of life and eternal life are predominant in the Gospel of John. How would you explain the second half of Jesus statement, *He who believes in me will live, even though he dies; and whoever lives and believes in me will never die?*

I Am the Way, the Truth, and the Life

John 14:1-31

Jesus said *I AM the way, and the truth and the life. No one comes to the Father except through me.* What a profound declaration, one that contradicts the world's view that "there are many ways to God." If we are to relate to our heavenly Father, there is no other way but Christ, no other truth but his, and no other life but his eternal flow.

The last two I AM statements of Christ occur during the final week in Jerusalem as part of the Upper Room Discourse. Spring has arrived in Palestine; Passover is at hand and Jesus and his disciples have returned to Jerusalem to celebrate the feast. Jesus has already received the triumphant "hosannas" from the people as he made his way into Jerusalem from the Mount of Olives. He has humbly washed the feet of his disciples. The treacherous Judas has departed the Passover meal in order to betray Jesus to the Jewish authorities. As the eleven remaining disciples lounge in his presence, Jesus brings further revelation as to his divinity.

These last two I AM statements are delivered only in the presence of his loyal disciples, not to the crowds that have previously surrounded him. Judas has left. The overriding theme of these two passages is relationship to Jesus and the Father, an association exclusive to the believer alone.

The Passover meal has been eaten, and the disciples are reclining around the ceremonial table. Jesus begins to prepare these men for his imminent departure by speaking words of encouragement to them. His conversation centers upon unity in his relationship to the Father and the coming presence of the Holy Spirit. He desires to reveal the true nature of his heavenly Father so that his disciples may grasp the immense love of their heavenly Father.

17. Jesus is concerned with the heart condition and well-being of his disciples. In verse 1 and 27 the word *tarasso* is used for troubled and means to cause one inward commotion, take away his calmness of mind, disturb his equanimity, to disquiet, make restless.[102] Verse 27 also contains the word peace, the tranquil state of a soul assured of its salvation through Christ, and so fearing nothing from God and content with its earthly lot.[103]

A. According to verse 1, why should the disciples' hearts be at rest?

B. What promises does Jesus make to his disciples to reassure them?

Verse 2

Verse 7

Verse 12 -The word great (*megas*) in verse 12 means much quantity, much in degree, great in size, or important.[104]

Verse 14

Verse 16-18

Verse 27

C. How is the peace Jesus gives different from the peace of the world?

18. Jesus answered, *I am the way and the truth and the life. No one comes to the Father except through me. If you really know me, you will know my Father as well. From now on, you do know him and have seen him.* (John 14:6-7) As Jesus prepares to leave, he comforts his disciples with revelation of the Father. What do these verses indicate and illustrate about the Father?

Verse 10

Verse 20

Verse 21

Verse 23

I Am the True Vine

John 15:1-16:4

Leaving the site of the Passover meal, it is quite possible that Jesus and his disciples passed by the great golden vine on the front of the temple.[105] This national emblem of Israel served as a symbol of Israel tracing its roots back to the Old Testament scriptures in Psalms and Isaiah. Using this as a striking metaphor, Jesus expounds upon his role as the only true vine, the source and vehicle to supply and sustain their spiritual life. The Father is the one who tends the vine by shaping and cutting the branches. The role of the disciples is to stay connected in order to receive the rich, vibrant spiritual flow that will produce fruit.

As he continues his parting instructions, Jesus elevates the position of his disciples from that of a servant, to that of a friend. The ramifications of their new relationship will be evident in the near future as they partner with the Holy Spirit to spread the good news. Throughout the book of Acts, the disciples preach the gospel message energized with the foundation of this new relationship—agape love.

Jesus speaks somber words as he warns his disciples of future persecution. Because *the servant is not greater than the master*, his disciples will be treated in much the same way that He has been received. In this passage, the world refers to the mass of unbelievers who are indifferent or hostile to God and his people. The perfect tense of the verb, to hate (*miseo*), implies that the world's hatred is a fixed attitude toward him and will carry over to the disciples as well.[106] Their new relationship to Jesus as friend carries with it a negative side. They have been called out of the world and the world will hate them.

The Vine and Vineyard

The vine was noted for its luxuriant foliage, intertwining branches, and trailing or climbing shoots. Grapes were eaten fresh, dried into raisin clusters, and the juice was boiled down into thick syrup. But wine, or "new wine," was the chief product.

Vineyards were commonly planted on hillsides, which were less suitable for grain cultivation, though they were also established in the major valleys and plains. The Hebron area was especially noted for its grapes, as was Sibmah in Transjordan. An annual vintage festival was held at Shiloh.

Vineyards required long-term intensive care. The soil was first dug and cleared of stones and a wall (or hedge) erected to discourage predators. A watchtower and wine vat completed the installation, with a booth for lodging during the harvest. Vines required heavy annual pruning, hoeing, thinning and support of fruit clusters, and sometimes irrigation. Intensive labor heightened expectations of the harvest and made loss of the vintage a bitter disappointment.

In the Bible text, flourishing vineyards meant peacetime; a ravaged vineyard represented war's devastation. This was characterized in scripture by broken walls, vines choked by thorns, and branches trampled by wild beasts. Restoration was represented by a time of planting vineyards and drinking their wine.[107]

19. The word remain (*meno*) occurs eleven times in this chapter. It carries the connotation to stay, remain, abide, wait for, remain in place or state, continue to exist, continue in an activity or state.[108]

A. What exactly needs to remain in these verses?

Verse 4

Verse 7

Verse 9

B. What is the end result of remaining in the vine (verses 7-8)?

C. What does Jesus promise to those who remain in him and his word (verse7)?

20. One aspect that is emphasized in this account is the role of the gardener in keeping the branch fruitful. He cuts off (*aireo*) meaning to lift up or take away. He prunes and makes clean (*kathaireo*) or purifies and cleanses.[109]

A. What does the gardener cut off and why (verse 2)?

B. What does the gardener prune and why (verse 2)?

C. How does the gardener prune the branches (verse 3)?

21. Jesus instructs his disciples to remain in his love in order to bear fruit.

A. What is the prerequisite for remaining in his love (verse 10)?

B. What is the result of remaining in his love according to verse 11?

C. The new command Jesus leaves with his disciples is to _____
_____(verse 17).

22. The disciples are promoted by Jesus from servants (*doulos*, a slave, bondman, man of servile condition, one who gives himself up to another's will.)[110]

A. How does Jesus distinguish between a servant and a friend (verse 15)?

B. In verse 16, Jesus chooses (*eklegomai*, to choose out, to pick out,to pick or choose out for one's self[111]) and appoints (*tithemei*, to set, fix establish, to set forth, ordain[112]) his disciples. What is his primary motivation for choosing them?

Persecution

Persecution came from two distinct sources...the Jews and the Romans. Stephen's preaching in Acts turned public opinion and brought about the first persecution in Jerusalem. In 44 A.D., Herod Agrippa executed James, and throughout Acts, the Jews appear as Paul's most vehement enemies. The Apostolic Council that repudiated the need for circumcision could only have made this attitude worse. The persecution culminated in the excommunication of Christians at Jamnia in 80 A.D.

Rome's forbearing attitude also underwent a marked change. At first, Rome gave Christians toleration and even encouragement. This soon gave way to fierce opposition. In Rome, the Christians became so unpopular that Nero made them scapegoats for the fire in 64 A.D. By 112 A.D. in Bithynia Christianity was a capital offence.[113]

23. The previous section speaks so strongly of love and abiding in the love of God. Now it is contrasted to hate, a hate that is tangible and vindictive. Jesus promises a life no different from his own.

A. Who does the world hate (verse 23-25)?

B. Record the three reasons why the world will hate Jesus' disciples.

Verse19

Verse 21

Verse 22

C. Why does he take the time to warn his disciples before the persecution starts (16:1)?

Making It Personal

In this chapter, we have examined the various I AMs of Christ. Each of these names carries a promise of his provision and care for us. As the Bread of Life he sustains and feeds our souls. As the Light of the World he illuminates our darkened understanding and sheds light to guide our way. As the Gate, he guards our going out and coming in. As the Good Shepherd, he nurtures, guides, protects, and tends our soul. As the Resurrection and Life he provides a life link to the heavenly and eternal life flow. As the Way, Truth, and Life he points the path forward. As the True Vine, he guarantees joy, fruitfulness, and lasting significance by allowing his life to become ours.

At the age of twenty-nine, Jesus became my liberator and healer. At the moment of salvation, the power of sin was broken over my life, but the sanctification process had only just begun. I have since experienced the awesome power of our Lord to liberate in a variety of fashions. Sometimes the freedom came with a simple request; other times by meditating on the word. God has touched me when others have prayed for me and even during worship as a sovereign act. This I know—God is still liberating his people and able *to set at liberty them that are bruised.* (Luke 4:18).

What are your needs today? Where do you need freedom? Where do you need nurture? Where do you need guidance? As the great I AM, Christ is more than able to meet every need.

24. When I first became a Christian, I thought that the more I did and the harder I worked, then the more Christ-like and pleasing to God I became. I was performance oriented. Because my self esteem was low, I felt I needed to earn the approval of God. I eventually had to reject that lie and realize that God accepts me just like I am.

   A. Have you ever felt driven to peform in order to prove your worth?

   B. What was the result?

   C. How can you overcome the desire to prove your self-worth?

25. Godly shepherds are a blessing in the Body of Christ! Although each may have his or her human imperfections, they each strive to fulfill the call of God on their lives. They have a demanding position, one that requires a complete commitment to God. Take a moment to consider the demands and challenges of your shepherd.

   A. List some characteristics you admire in the man or woman of God who is your pastor.

   B. How can you support their efforts in the ministry?

   C. Consider some ways to demonstrate your appreciation for your shepherd. Record your ideas and follow through on at least one of them.

26. Just as the disciples are chosen and appointed to bear fruit, we also have that same command from Jesus.

   A. In what ways do we remain connected to the vine?

   B. How does today's Christian bear fruit for the kingdom of God? In what ways have you borne fruit or hope to bear fruit?

C. Record a time when you felt "pruned" by the hand of God. What effect did it ultimately have?

27. Which of the I AMs do you need in your present circumstances? Find a scripture that reflects the nature of God towards you in that area and spend time each day meditating on it. (Meditating is to repeat the scripture often. Then stop and reflect on what that scripture says to you).

Jesus,

Thank you for showing me the beauty and fullness of your divine nature. I want to know you and experience the provision of the great I AM. Help me to grasp the vast meaning of your many names and how they apply to my life.

Thank you for your power and strength to embrace the new nature and resist the old. I submit myself to you as a branch that needs to be tended and pruned. I desire, Lord, to bear much fruit for your kingdom. Please show me how to remain in Jesus the Vine, how to remain in his love, and how to remain in his word. Thank you for your tender care of me, a branch in your vineyard.

Amen

Notes

Chapter Seven

The Final Hours

*H*ow would you spend your last week on earth? With family or friends? Would you take that one last vacation, buy the car you always wanted, travel to some exotic destination? What would your parting words and actions be—reflections of fond memories, incisive wisdom gleaned through your life experiences, or encouragement to those who would be left behind? As Jesus approaches his final days on earth, he chooses to spend his closing hours in close fellowship with friends and the disciples who love him. He awaits the Passover celebration, the exact timing for his ultimate sacrifice when he will become the Passover lamb for the entire nation.

Jesus is Honored

John 12:1-50

In Chapter 12, John describes two occasions where Jesus is honored before his betrayal and death. The first is at a banquet in Bethany, the site of Lazarus' restoration. Although this is a few months after their brother's resurrection, it may be the first opportunity Martha and Mary have had to show their gratitude to Jesus. Martha is busy serving the guests, and Mary is about to demonstrate her love and appreciation for Jesus in a way that will forever hail her as an ardent follower of Christ. Mary's extravagant act of anointing Jesus' feet may be considered improper and an intrusion, but she is motivated by a deep appreciation for the man she knows as friend and Lord.

Jesus is honored for a second time in Chapter 12 during his triumphal entry into Jerusalem. Riding on a young donkey, Jesus makes his way across the Mount of Olives. With palm branches waving and Hosannas echoing across the hillside, the people welcome their king into Jerusalem.

This significant event is better understood against the background of the excitement and pageantry that accompanied the Passover celebrations. The attendance in Jerusalem approached three million, with the masses ready for any excitement. Many pilgrims lived in tents in the surrounding areas, so there would have been many travelers close to the route Jesus followed from Bethany. A crowd of some tens of thousands could have participated in the triumphal entry.

Jerusalem's inhabitants traditionally welcomed the arriving pilgrims with an antiphonal chant based on Psalm 118:25–28. Jerusalemites would chant the first half of each of these verses, while the arriving pilgrims responded with the last half, and in unison they would sing verse 29, concluding with Psalm 103:17. The chant that echoed back and forth across the Kidron Valley, east of Jerusalem, that afternoon was as follows:

Hosanna!

Hosanna to the Son of David!

Blessed is He who comes in the name of the Lord!

Blessed is the King who comes in the name of the Lord!

The King of Israel!

Blessed is the Kingdom of Our Father David, that comes in the name of the Lord!

Peace in Heaven and glory in the highest! Hosanna in the highest![114]

The message of Christ, his every word and deed, has been in accordance to the commandments of the Father. Jesus has not spoken a word that the Father has not given him to speak, nor has he performed any miraculous sign that the Father did not pre-approve. As he stands in the midst of a divided throng, Jesus proclaims his obedience to the Father as a final witness to his life. He will now withdraw from the public eye in preparation for his pending crucifixion.

Ointments and Perfumes

Soft unguents or salves and aromatic scents were commonly used in the ancient Near East for anointing, for medicinal purposes, for beautification, in incense, and for embalming. Most ointments contained a base of olive oil, to which aromatic spices, especially myrrh, were added.

Archaeological excavation has brought to light a great variety of small delicate flasks and jars that undoubtedly served as containers for cosmetics, ointments, and perfumes. The most precious containers were of alabaster and were often small jars with a lid and pedestal base, or vials with a sealed neck.

Anointing the head with oil was a common form of hospitality. Ointments were a precious commodity and symbolized a sacred consecration. Kings were anointed, as was the tabernacle. Ointments were also used for healing and for perfume.

Perfumes were likewise regarded as precious and served not only cosmetic uses but were also a main ingredient of incense and the sacred anointing oil. Often referred to as spices, aromatic sources were derived from plants such as frankincense, myrrh, cinnamon, and saffron. Fragrances made women attractive, provided a pleasing scent to clothes, and furniture, and flavored wine. The blending of several perfumes was an important component of formulas for the sacred incense and anointing oil.[115]

1. Jesus is the honored guest in Bethany, just a short distance from Jerusalem. As the men recline around the tables, leaning on cushions with one arm and eating with the other, Mary demonstrates her devotion to Christ with an extravagant act.

A. Spikenard is a perfume imported from India and extracted from a Himalayan plant. History records this perfume as a gift exchanged between kings, a rare and costly token of appreciation. It is usually sealed in an alabaster cruse, and when the seal is broken the rich fragrance permeates every corner of the house in which it is released. At a very special banquet, the host uses one container of oil to anoint all of his guests.[116]How does Mary honor Jesus during this special dinner and how does this generous gift reflect her inner convictions?

B. Judas reacts in quite a different manner, objecting vehemently to her ministrations. What is his primary concern about Mary's anointing of Jesus?

C. How does Jesus respond?

2. The miracle of raising Lazarus from the dead continues to stir reactions from the religious rulers and the masses.

    A. Why do the Jews travel to Bethany (verse 9)?

    B. What is the consequence of their trip (verse 11,17)?

    C. How do the chief priests retaliate toward Jesus and Lazarus (verse 10)?

3. As Passover approaches, Jesus and his disciples travel from Bethany into Jerusalem. It is common for Passover celebrants to arrive early for the feast to ensure their ceremonial purity and to secure lodging that becomes scarce as the festival days approach.

    A. How do the people honor Jesus as he enters Jerusalem (verse 13)?

    B. How do the disciples react (verse 16)?

4. In his last public conversation, Jesus identifies this Passover celebration as the appointed time of the Father for his sacrifice. Knowing what lies before him, Jesus realizes that he could ask the Father to save him, but his intent is to once more glorify his heavenly Father.

    A. What does the Father state he will do (verse 28)?

    B. There are three occasions where the gospels record an audible voice from heaven. In each instance it is a divine endorsement of Jesus, his authority, and Sonship. Record each occasion in these scriptures and the words spoken about Jesus.

        Matthew 3:17

        Mark 9:7

        John 12:28-29 27

    C. What metaphor does Jesus use to explain his coming death (verse 24)?

C. What traits characterize someone who is a servant of God (verse 25-26)?

5. Many are still divided in their understanding of who Jesus is. Appealing to Old Testament scripture, John provides editorial comment as to why many did not believe in Jesus as the Messiah. In verse 40, the word blinded (*typhloo*) is defined as to make not to understand, cause blindness, deprive of sight.[117] The word for hardened (*poroo*) is to have a closed mind, harden, make dull. [118]

A. Why do many of the people still not believe (verse 40)?

B. Many of the leaders believe, but what prevents them from openly acknowledging Jesus as the Son of God (verse 42-43)?

The Last Supper

John 13:1-38

Passover is at hand; the room has been secured; the meal has been prepared. The stage is set for the definitive betrayal by Judas that activates Jesus' trial, crucifixion, and resurrection. Jesus and his disciples gather in Jerusalem for what would become known as The Last Supper.

The room acquired for the dinner is on the second floor of a house, the Upper Room. It is usually the largest in the dwelling. The seating arrangements at this banquet consist of a low table about 12x15 feet with cushions for each diner. The men position themselves in a u-shape format around the table, feet stretched out behind them. Judas reclines on one side of Christ, John at the other, with Peter lounging across the table from the three. Two-thirds of the table is covered with a cloth, and one third exposed for the serving vessels. The Passover elements of the four cups of wine, bitter herbs, salt water, unleavened bread, charoset (mixture of nuts, wine, and fruit), and the lamb itself are brought out during the ceremony.[119]

With the burden of his upcoming death pressing upon him, Jesus serves his followers and expresses the full measure of his perfect, steadfast love. With deep humility, Jesus teaches them by his actions that they are not to emulate the world's standards of greatness, but God's. He stoops to perform an act of common servitude reserved for the lowest of the household servants...he washes the feet of his the disciples. Like a father with his adolescent children, he patiently takes the time to explain his ministrations knowing he will soon be gone from their presence. The fledgling ministers of the gospel are encouraged by Jesus to imitate his actions. They are to humble themselves in service by deferring to one another.

Though the disciples are unaware of Judas' deception, Jesus has always known Judas would betray him. In spite of this, Jesus sits beside Judas, washes his feet, and continues with the Passover celebration. It is no wonder the eleven are surprised by Jesus' declaration of betrayal. Even at the last decisive moment, Jesus still offers his love and a choice to Judas. As the defector departs, John eloquently states *it was night*, for the spiritual darkness that Jesus had spoken of many times before has begun.

With the departure of Judas, the eleven stand pure and cleansed in the company of their Master and Lord. The purity of the group and the finality of the hour direct Jesus' conversation to more intimate topics of discussion. What Jesus could not and would not share in the company of Judas, he now discloses openly to the trusted few who remain.

The Passover Ritual

The Passover celebration typically followed this order:

1. An opening benediction by the host, "Blessed art Thou, Jehovah our God, Who has created the fruit of the Vine!"

2. The First Cup-A cup of wine mixed with water was circulated and all drank from it.

3. The master of the feast took a basin of water to each person, who, by rinsing his hands in it, ceremonially cleansed himself. (This was additional to, and subsequent to, the regular ritual washing before a meal. Some believe it was at this point that Jesus chose instead to wash the feet of his disciples.)

4. The Passover lamb and other courses of the feast were laid on the table.

5. The feast master dipped a bundle of herbs into the salt water, spoke a blessing, and handed the bitter herbs to all, who ate these as a reminder of their past bondage in Egypt and their present bondage to sin.

6. A second benediction was given and more bitter herbs were eaten. One of the unleavened cakes is broken in two. Half is placed on a dish, elevated, and these words spoken: "This is the bread of misery which our fathers ate in the land of Egypt. All that are hungry, come and eat; all that are needy, come, keep the Pascha." The other half is put aside until after supper and called the Afikomen.

7. The Second Cup- The wine cup was circulated for the second time.

8. The questions prescribed by Moses in Exodus 12:26 were asked by the youngest.

9. The first half of the "Songs of Hallel" was sung (Psalms 113–114).

10. All washed their hands. The feast master prepared sops (by wrapping herbs and lamb in unleavened bread), dipped them in sauce and gave them to participants.

11. Everyone then ate.

12. Hands were washed for the third time.

13. The Third Cup-The wine cup, the Cup of Blessing, was circulated for the third time. The Afikomen is broken and offered to participants of the meal. Many believe this was the institution of the Lord's Supper. [226]

14. The concluding benedictory prayer was said.

15. The Fourth Cup-The feast concluded with the circulation of the wine cup for the fourth time.

16. The second half of the Hallel was sung (Psalms 115–118 plus portions from Isaiah). [120]

6. Knowing his time is short, Jesus purposefully shows his disciples the full extent of his love.

   A. According to John 13:3, what is the foundation for Jesus' strength of character and purpose?

   B. How does he demonstrate his love for the disciples?

   C. What virtues are modeled by Jesus for his disciples?

7. Simon Peter, sitting opposite Jesus, is probably the first to have his feet washed. He struggles with his Master performing such a menial task for him.

   A. Why does Simon Peter refuse to have his feet washed by Jesus?

   B. From the Greek meros, the phrase *to have a part in* (verse 8) refers to get as a share, to have a share in.[121] Why is it imperative for Peter to have his feet washed?

   C. Jesus proclaims his disciples to be clean (verse 10), from the Greek word *katharos* signifying clean, pure, free from corrupt desire, from sin and guilt, sincere, genuine.[122] Yet they need cleansing from the daily dirt and dust of their travels. Salvation is also both a total immersion into the life of Christ and an ongoing process. How would you compare the constant sanctification process with the foot-washing ceremony?

   D. What does Jesus ask of his disciples with reference to the foot-washing (verse14-17)?

Judas Iscariot

As one of the twelve apostles, the son of Simon Iscariot, Judas was possibly the only apostle from Judea. Judas possessed a privileged position among the apostles as treasurer of the group. His proximity to Jesus at the Lord's Supper also suggests this.

\Why he betrayed Jesus is uncertain. Some suggest that he did it after being convinced that Jesus truly planned to die; or that he did it for money.

Despite a loving gesture by Jesus during the last supper, Judas proceeded to betray his Lord in Gethsemane by singling him out at night with a kiss. Upon reflecting over what he had done, Judas experienced remorse and sought to undo his evil deed, but it was not possible. In sorrow he hanged himself perhaps over the valley of Hinnom, "and the rope giving way, or the branch to which he hung breaking, he fell down headlong on his face, and was crushed and mangled on the rocky pavement below." (Matthew 26:48-49, 27:3-5, Acts 1:18-19)Judas was chosen to be an apostle, even though Jesus knew from the beginning who should betray him.[123]

8. With Judas reclining at his side, Jesus quotes from Psalm 41:9. Judas' betrayal that is about to take place will fulfill the Old Testament scripture. The word for betray is *paradidomi*, to give into the hands of another; to deliver up one to custody, to be judged, condemned, punished, scourged, tormented, put to death; to deliver up treacherously.[124]

A. What is the nature of Jesus' relationship with Judas according to Psalm 41:9?

B. Why is Jesus telling the remaining eleven before the betrayal happens (verse 19 ends with I AM)?

C. The word *lambano* means to receive what is offered, not to refuse or reject, to receive a person, give him access to one's self.[125] It is used four times as receive in verse 20. What realistic truth does Jesus impart to his disciples?

D. How does yielding to temptation affect Judas Iscariot (verse 27)?

9. Jesus has followed the commandments of God his entire life. Now, at the commencement of he Church, he institutes one of his own decrees.

A. What new command does Jesus give his disciples (verse 34)?

B. How will this be significant in the establishment of the Church (verse 35)?

10. Peter is the impulsive disciple, speaking boldly both to his detriment and his benefit. In this case, he vehemently professes he will give his life for Jesus, only to be reprimanded by Jesus who foresees the events of the future.

A. How does Jesus chastise Peter's rash statement (verse 38)?

B. How would you compare Peter's pending denial to Judas' betrayal? How are they the same? How are they different?

The Holy Spirit

John 14:15-27, 16:5-16

From Genesis through the prophets, the Spirit of God has been at work on the earth. The Old Testament contains numerous references to the Holy Spirit, Spirit of the Lord, or the Spirit of God. The term spirit is translated from the Hebrew *ruach* and Greek *pneuma*, words denoting wind and breath. With the adjective "holy," the reference is to the divine spirit, the Spirit of God.

Three major emphases may be identified in the Old Testament. The first is the Holy Spirit as an agent in creation. The second emphasis is the Holy Spirit as God's presence in the covenantal community. The third is the Holy Spirit as a source of inspiration and power. In these instances, the Holy Spirit becomes a vehicle of God's revelation and activity.

Israel's leaders—from Moses to Joshua, to the judges, to David and Solomon—all receive their wisdom, courage, and power as gifts resulting from God's Spirit. The primary example, however, is surely the inspiration of the prophets, who, because they possess this Spirit, speak and act with an authority and power not their own.

Along with the Old Testament prophecies relating to the Holy Spirit, the New Testament promises a fresh, vibrant relationship with the third member of the Godhead. In Chapter 14, 15, and 16 in the Gospel of John, Jesus reassures the disciples that they will not be left alone. When he has departed, the Father will send another *Paraclete* to enact growth in the Church and the maturation of the saints.

In the New Testament, the Holy Spirit empowers the church for its mission. This idea comes to fullest expression in John 14, where the Holy Spirit is described as an Advocate (Counselor, Helper, Paraclete) who represents both divine presence and guidance for the disciples. In keeping with this, the Holy Spirit comes to represent both the presence and activity of God and the continuing presence of Jesus Christ in the church.[126]

The Holy Spirit in the Old Testament

Despite the strong influence of the Holy Spirit in the Old Testament, there are some slight differences in the manifestation of his work. The following characteristics differentiate the working of God's Spirit in the Old Testament from the New Testament indwelling of the believer:

1. The Holy Spirit "rested upon" a person or group. He did not dwell within them.

2. There was a generally a specific purpose to accomplish.

3. The presence of the Holy Spirit was not a sanctifying influence.

4. The presence of the Holy Spirit was not proportionate to one's spirituality.

5. The presence of the Holy Spirit was temporary. It could be lifted, as with King Saul.

6. The presence of the Holy Spirit was the extension of the power and authority of God.

7. The presence of the Holy Spirit was a sovereign gift of God, not a gift of grace.

8. Kings, priests, prophets, and select groups experienced the anointing of the Holy Spirit in the Old Testament.

11. What does the Apostle John document about the Holy Spirit in these scriptures?

John 3:5

John 3:34

John 6:63

John 7:38-39

John 14:16-17

12. Jesus tells his disciples the Father will send another Counselor to be with them forever. With this statement, Jesus acknowledges the similarity between his purpose on earth and the Holy Spirit's role. The word Counselor or *parakletos* means comforter, advocate, called to one's side, called to one's aid, an intercessor, a helper, succorer, assistant. The Holy Spirit is destined to take the place of Christ, to lead the disciples to a deeper knowledge of the gospel truth, and to give them divine strength needed to undergo trials and persecutions on behalf of the divine kingdom.[127]What are the different names Jesus uses for the Holy Spirit?

John 14:16-17

John 15:26

John 16:7

John 16:13

13. Referencing the words of Jesus in Chapters 14, 15, and 16 what is the function of the Holy Spirit in the lives of his disciples?

John 14:26

1.

2.

John 15:26

John 16:13-14

   1.

   2.

   3.

   4.

14. In John 16:8-11, Jesus outlines the convicting work of the Holy Spirit. The Greek word for convict (*elegcho*) means to rebuke, expose, refute, show one's fault.[128] What are the three areas of conviction the Holy Spirit brings?

   1.

   2.

   3.

15. The arrival of the Holy Spirit on the Feast of Pentecost marks a decided change in the demeanor and actions of the disciples.

   A. What unique manifestations characterize this spiritual milestone for the infant Church (Acts 1:2-4)?

   B. In Acts 1:8, Jesus solidifies the purpose for the Holy Spirit's presence within a believer. What is that purpose?

   C. Acts 2:14-41 describes Peter's initial response to the unction of the Holy Spirit. How does the indwelling of the Holy Spirit change Peter from the man he was only days before?

   D. How does the Holy Spirit continue to be involved in the life of believers according to these scriptures?

1 Corinthians 2:10-16

Romans 15:19

1 Corinthians 12:6, 11

Acts 13:2

Acts 16:6, 7, 10

Pentecost

The festival, its name meaning "the fiftieth," is first spoken of in Exodus 23:16 as "the feast of harvest," and again in Exodus 34:22 as "the day of the firstfruits." From the sixteenth of the month of Nisan (the second day of the Passover), seven complete weeks, or forty-nine days, were to be counted, and this feast was held on the fiftieth day.[129]

The feast was proclaimed as a holy convocation on which no servile work was to be done, and at which every male Israelite was required to appear at the sanctuary.

Two baked loaves of new, fine, leavened flour were brought out of the dwellings and waved by the priest before the Lord, together with the offerings of animal sacrifice for sin and peace-offerings. As a day of joy, the devout Israelite expressed gratitude for the blessings of the grain harvest and experienced heartfelt fear of the Lord.[130]

The Lord's Prayer

John 17:1-26

Jesus' parting comments to his disciples are found in the last half of Chapter 16 (verses 16-33). He speaks obscurely to his disciples and they wonder what he means by *In a little while you will see me no more, and then after a little while you will see me*. The fact that they "kept asking" shows their bewilderment at what is about to take place. Jesus concludes his instructions by telling the disciples they will scatter and desert him, adding to their confusion. Yet, even the midst of the coming turmoil, Jesus leaves them with a promise of hope—he gives them his peace.

Although they are still confused about the nature of his remarks and the clarity of their meaning, the disciples are resolved to trust in their Master and believe his words wholeheartedly.

As the final blessing to those who are his own, Jesus offers his concluding prayer. What some refer to as "the high priestly prayer" is actually a review and consolidation of Jesus' many teachings. These few verses condense the heart of his ministry, his purpose, and his hope for the future of the Church.

The chapter is divisible into three parts:

1) Jesus' prayer concerning himself (1-5)

2) His prayer for the disciples (6-19)

3) His prayer for all believers present and future (20-26).

The petition was spoken just before the group left the Upper Room and made their way across the Kidron Valley to Gethsemane. It is characterized by John's familiar use of the words glory, glorify, sent, believe, world, and love. It is exclusive to the Gospel of John.[131]

The prayer of Jesus begins with *the time has come*. Throughout this gospel timing has been of great importance. Jesus informed his mother in Cana that his *time had not yet come* (2:4), nevertheless he still changes the water to wine. When his brothers urge him to present himself in Jerusalem to gain publicity (7:8), *the right time had not come*. Twice Jesus escapes death at the hands of an angry mob because his *time had not come*(7:30, 8:20). But now the hour has arrived (12:23, 13:31) for him to return to the Father.

With the realization that his disciples would soon fail him, Jesus offers prayer on their behalf to the Father. He holds a great confidence that these same followers who will momentarily scatter in fear will one day stand strong as preachers of the gospel message. Consider the impact of his final prayer in the minds and hearts of these disciples.

As Jesus closes in prayer, his thoughts go beyond those eleven men who stand before him. With omniscient awareness, he sees the multitude of believers who will one day be part of the kingdom of God. Moved with compassion, his intercession for the future Church has a single focus—unity.

Prayer

Prayer is simply a conversation with God. It may be aloud or mental, occasional or constant, formal or informal. Prayer should be offered with faith that God is, and is the hearer and answerer of prayer, and that he will fulfill his word (Hebrews 11:6).

There are no rules anywhere in Scripture for the manner of prayer or the position to be assumed. There is mention made of kneeling in prayer, of bowing and falling prostrate, of spreading out the hands, and of standing. Excluding the "Lord's Prayer" (Mathew 6:9–13) which is a model or pattern of prayer, there is no special form of prayer for general use given in Scripture.[132]

Prayer is to be offered using the name of Christ. To pray in the name of Jesus is to pray in the authority of Christ himself. For Jesus the true focus in prayer was the Father's will. He prayed in secret, in times of spiritual conflict, and on the cross. In his prayers he offered thanksgiving, sought guidance, interceded, and communed with the Father. The burden of his high priestly prayer in John 17 is the unity of the church. According to Romans 8:34, he always lives to intercede in behalf of the saints.[133]

16. Referencing the birth of a child (verse 21) as first a time of grief and then supreme joy, Christ tries to prepare his disciples for his imminent departure. The ominous language in verse 32 (*The time is coming and has come.*) is a prelude to the dramatic events about to unfold.

A. Jesus predicts two things in verse 32. Record what he foresees happening to his relationship with the disciples.

B. The word for trouble is *thlipsis* meaning a pressing, pressing together, pressure, oppression, affliction, tribulation, distress, straits.[134] Where will the disciples have peace (verse 33)? Where will they have trouble?

C. To overcome (*nikao*) is to conquer, overcome, overpower, prevail, triumph, and be victorious.[135] What do you think Jesus means when he says he has overcome the world?

17. The theme of glory and glorifying is prevalent in these first few verses of his prayer in Chapter 17. The Greek word is *doxazomai* (the noun) and *doxazo* (the verb). It means praise, honor, to attribute high status or rank, be wonderful, be of exceptional value.[136]

A. What is Jesus' request? How will this be accomplished?

B. In reference to verse 3, what scriptural definition does Jesus apply to eternal life?

C. According to verse 4, how has Jesus already brought glory to the Father?

18. Jesus prays for his disciples, the ones entrusted to him by the Father for a time of teaching and training.

A. What truths have the disciples learned at the feet of their Master Jesus?

Verse 7

Verse 8a

Verse 8b

B. To protect (*tereo*) is to keep on, guard, keep watch over, obey[137] and is used in verse 11 and 15. To keep safe (*phylassomai*) is to guard closely, watch, keep in custody, obey[138] and is used in verse 12. Although the words can be used as synonyms, *tereo* has the sense of protection by conservation; *phylassomai* is protection from external attack.[139]

What specific request does Jesus make to the Father in verse 11?

In verse 15, what is his plea?

C. The word sanctify used in verses 17 and 19 is *hagazio* and is best defined as a two-fold process—separation from the world and separation unto God.[140] In verse 17, the verb tense is aorist imperative that speaks of an initial complete separation. In verse 19, the tense is perfect passive that indicates a fixed and final state.[141] How will the disciples be sanctified (verse 17)?

19. Webster's Dictionary defines unity as a condition of harmony, accord, continuity without deviation or change, the quality or state of being made one.[142]

A. The unity Jesus describes has two components. In verse 21, what two aspects of unity does Jesus describe?

1.

2.

B. Why does Jesus pray for this kind of unity to take place? (verse 21, 23)

20. On the brink of his crucifixion, what final request does Jesus ask of his heavenly Father? (verse 24)

Making It Personal

There are two fundamental distinctions between Christianity and other religions. First, the founder of the faith, Jesus Christ, is still very much alive. Jesus defeated death, hell, and the grave and lives at the right hand of the Father. The heads of other spiritual movements have expired—Mohammad is dead. Joseph Smith has expired. Gautama the Buddha has been entombed. Confucius has passed away. Only their decaying remains are left behind. In contrast to these ancient founders of their faith, the garden tomb is empty!

Second, the ministry of the Holy Spirit separates Christianity from other spiritual beliefs. What other faith has a Paraclete, a Helper, Counselor, and Teacher that comes from God himself to abide with his children? The Holy Spirit is sent specifically to the Church; the world cannot comprehend him. His mission is to assist believers, dwell among and in them, and strengthen the body of Christ.

As a non-believer many years ago, I had never heard of the third member of the Trinity, the Holy Spirit.

I was familiar with God the Father and his Son Jesus. I enjoyed Biblically-based movies like *The Ten Commandments*, *The Greatest Story Ever Told*, and *Ben Hur*. I had memorized scriptures in Vacation Bible School and even entertained local churches with a drama group. But who was this Holy Spirit?

My godly neighbor spoke constantly of the Holy Spirit. He was a real person to her—he communicated, taught, guided decisions, helped in the daily routine of her life, empowered her prayers. This "spirit" who enabled her to live such a joyful, peace-filled lifestyle intrigued me. I needed someone to help me! I was motivated to investigate further and discovered for myself the precious relationship available with the Holy Spirit.

Through the ministry and ongoing presence of the Holy Spirit, I am empowered to live like Christ and for him. It is the Holy Spirit who constantly shows me how much God really cares, how much he is concerned and desires to be a part of my life. He motivates me to pray, to give, to love, and obey heavenly directives.

As you complete these reflective questions, remember the role of the Holy Spirit in each expression of your Christian walk.

21. Recall the various attributes of the Holy Spirit and how he works in the life of believers.

    A. How do you see the Holy Spirit at work in your life?

    B. In what ways would you like to know the Holy Spirit more intimately?

    C. The word states, *Draw near to God and he will draw near to you.*(James 4:8) List some ways in which you could draw closer to God.

    D. You may have discovered a deep desire within you to know more about the Holy Spirit. What does Luke 11:13 affirm about receiving the Holy Spirit?

22. Jesus demonstrates love and humility to his disciples by washing their feet. In a similar fashion, God asks us to express the very same ideals as we interact with others. The word of God states, *He resists the proud, but gives grace to the humble.*(James 4:6) Humility, therefore, is a key element to successful Christian living. Humility before God is admitting you are lacking; humility before brothers and sisters in Christ is acknowledging your own imperfections and relying on their individual strengths. This kind of meekness is rooted in the love of God. True Christian love emanates from the heart of the Father, blossoms in the heart of his children, and manifests in the life of a vibrant Christian community. This is Jesus' mandate to his followers—to love one another.

    A. What role does foot-washing have for today's Christian?

    B. How can you demonstrate the love and humility of Jesus in your everyday life?

C. What impact would your actions have on those around you?

23. Giving, whether it is time, talent, or money, can reveal much about a person's character.

A. Can you recall a time when you, like Mary, gave extravagantly of yourself and resources? Record this occasion.

B. In what ways did this gift affect you? In what ways did it affect the recipients?

24. Prayers never die or fade away. In fact, the words we speak are infinite and carry tremendous spiritual power beyond the limited understanding of human beings. If you have ever studied the science of sound, you may have discovered that words produce sound waves that continue into infinity. Applying that scientific principle to Jesus sanctifying prayer, his words are ever resounding throughout his Creation. In essence, they are as powerful and productive today as they were when he first spoke them.

A. Which part of the Master's prayer was significant to you? Why?

B. Each of these scriptures describes a different aspect of prayer. How could you enrich your personal prayer time?

Ephesians 6:18

Philippians 4:6

1 Timothy 2:1-3

James 5:15

1 John 5:14-15

C. How successful are you walking in unity with your brothers and sisters in Christ?

D. How does unity differ from uniformity?

25. A constant theme throughout the gospel is the importance of the timing of the Lord. Is God's timing still relevant today? How can we discern and know the timing and seasons of God in our life?

Lord,

Thank you for your unconditional love. It is an anchor for my soul and a constant in my life. Even when I am confused and in the midst of turmoil, you are there as a comforting presence. Because you are love and your love is within me, I long to exhibit your divine unconditional love to others. I humble myself before you, God, and ask for your grace to love in new and greater ways. Open my eyes to your goodness and your many blessings that have come my way because of you.

Thank you that because of Jesus, I have access to your throne and your awesome splendor. As I come to you with my petitions, I thank you that you hear me and answer my prayers. Father, help me to come into unity in my family, in my church, and especially with you.

Your word says that those who hunger and thirst for righteousness will be filled. Lord, I hunger and thirst for more of you. I desire to see you move in my life like never before. I want to see your love, your grace, your power, and to know your will for my life. I long to be a dynamic witness for your kingdom, but I need your help. Please fill me with your Spirit. Fill every corner of my being and staurate me with your presence. I open myself to the fullness of your power.

(Pause and allow the presence of the Holy Spirit to touch you)

In Jesus name,

Amen

Notes

_____

_____

_____

_____

_____

_____

Chapter Eight

The Crucifixion, Resurrection, and Restoration

*E*arly one Easter morning, the sun barely cresting over the horizon, my family and I sat huddled beneath afghans on the cold, damp pavement in our church parking lot. It was our family tradition to attend Sunrise Service on Easter morning to honor the resurrection of the Lord. This particular Sunday morning was bone-chilling cold and we leaned against each other for any additional warmth that could be found.

The service began with resounding worship and praise followed by the pastor's Easter Resurrection message. As I sat listening to his inspirational words, I suddenly remembered the biblical concept of "laying on of hands." Used in the Old Testament and during the lifetime of Jesus, the "laying on of hands" transferred transgression and sin onto a "spotless" sacrificial animal. The responsible party placed his hands upon the animal, transferring his guilt and sin, and the animal was slain at the altar.

That morning the Holy Spirit began to reveal a new truth to me, one that always surfaces when I study the crucifixion. As Jesus passed from one group to another over those last 24 hrs, each touching his innocence with their sin-laden hands, their guilt was transferred to him. From commoners to elite, Romans to Jews, both secular and religious, they placed their hands upon him and the sin of the world was carried upon Jesus to the cross. Through betrayal, false accusations, outright lies and innuendos, Jesus bore the sin of a world that had rejected him.

This week as we study the ultimate sacrifice of the Lord Jesus Christ, remember that he not only carried our sin, but he conquered it. Jesus rose victoriously as the emissary of a new covenant, a covenant of salvation, healing, and restoration for generations to come.

Gethsemane and the Jewish Trial
John 18:1-27

As Jesus and his disciples leave their Passover meal and cross the Kidron Valley, they enter what John notes as "an olive grove." Known in the other gospel accounts as Gethsemane, the oil press,[143] it was a place frequented by Christ and his disciples. It is here that Christ himself will undergo a different kind of pressing.

In the Garden of Gethsemane, Jesus stands ready to fulfill all obedience to his heavenly Father and reverse Adam's curse upon mankind. In the Garden of Eden (Genesis 3), Adam disobeyed by succumbing to temptation and eating from the tree of the knowledge of good and evil. Sin was released into God's perfect creation. Triumphing as the *second Adam* (1 Corinthians 15:45), Jesus yields in obedience to the Father in the Garden of Gethsemane. *Not as I will, but as you will.* (Matthew 26:39) With this action, he reverses the disobedience of the first Adam in the Garden of Eden.

In the Garden of Gethsemane, the collusion between the Jewish authorities and the Roman officials begins to unfold. The Roman garrison in Jerusalem is a detachment of soldiers stationed at the Antonia Fortress adjacent to the Temple. During the Jewish festivals when crowds become rowdy, the Roman guard preserves the peace of the celebration. The chief priests and Pharisees possibly approach this military power with the insinuation that Jesus is a troublemaker and could instigate a riot.[144]

The Roman militia together with the religious leaders deliver Jesus to Annas, the ex-high priest The arrest of Jesus by the Roman guard initiates the trial portion of Christ's suffering and persecution. The Gospel of John is the only account that records delivering Jesus into the hands of Annas, the ex-high priest.

Annas

Annas was a well know figure in first-century Jewish history. He was considered successful, prosperous, and well respected as a former ex-high priest.

Annas held the office of high priest from 6-15 A.D. until he was deposed by the Roman curator Valerius Gratus. During the next twenty one years, the position was filled by five of his sons, his grandson, and son-in-law Caiaphas (18-36 A.D.). While they acted publicly, Annas was the "power behind the throne." He directed the religious affairs of Jerusalem without the restraints that the office imposed. His influence with the Romans was due to the religious views he held (he was a Sadducee), his open favor of the foreigners (contributing to his friends in the praetorium), and his enormous wealth extracted from the Temple exchanges.

The fact that Jesus was first brought to Annas, not the officiating high-priest Caiphas, in itself speaks of his stature with the Romans and in the Jewish hierarchy.[145]

1. Judas leads the group of men in search of Jesus. Many believe Gethsemane was a common resting place for Jesus and his disciples, a place of intimacy where Christ could gather with his own for refreshing and fellowship. Into this private arena Judas enters, a veritable second "snake" of the garden.

A. Who are the various groups of people accompanying Judas (verse 3)?

B. What does Mark 14:10-11 indicate about the collusion between Judas and the Jewish authorities?

C. How does Judas identify Jesus to the authorities (Luke 22:47-48)?

2. The mass of Pharisees, officials, and Roman soldiers declare they are seeking Jesus of Nazareth. In verses 5 and 8, Jesus' response was *I am he*, or once again in the Greek *ego eimi*—I AM.

A. What reaction do the people have to his declaration (verse 6)?

B. Knowing the certainty of what would soon happen to him, Jesus shows deep concern for his disciples. What do verses 4 and 8 indicate about this care?

3. The word cup (*poterion*) in verse 11 is a drinking vessel and also, metaphorically, one's lot or experience, whether joyous or adverse, divine appointments, whether favorable or unfavorable,

likened to a cup which God presents one to drink.[146] What cup has the Father assigned Jesus to drink in verse 11?

4. Two of the disciples, one named and one unnamed, follow Jesus as he is bound and taken to Annas.

A. Who are the two disciples?

B. The unnamed disciple receives preferential treatment in the household of the high priest. How is he favored and why (verse 15)?

5. The trial of Jesus before the Jewish religious leaders breaks tradition, as well as the Mosaic laws of justice for the following reasons: 1) Jesus is not formally tried and condemned by the Sanhedrin, but tried and sentenced in the palace of the high priest Caiaphas. 2) The proceedings commence at night in direct violation of Jewish law. 3) Judicial process is forbidden on the Sabbath or Feastdays or even the evening before. 4) The system of warning and cautionary witnesses in a capitol trial is ignored in this case.[147]

A. Read verses 20-23 that record Jesus' answers to the high priest. What impresses you the most about his answer?

B. One of the officials strikes Jesus in the face, an illegal act in any process of Jewish justice, especially when the accused is not condemned.[148] Why do you think this happens?

6. Only hours before, Jesus has prophesied Simon Peter's denial. Now in the pre-dawn hours of the morning, various people accost Peter with the question of his association to Jesus.

A. How does Peter demonstrate his defense of Jesus in the garden (verse 10)?

B. In contrast to his display of aggression in the garden, Peter denies Jesus three times. Who are the three people who challenge Peter's allegiance?

Verse 16-17

Verse 25

Verse 26-27

C. As the rooster crows heralding the rising sun, Peter denial is complete. What is his reaction when Jesus' prophecy is fulfilled (Luke 22:62)?

The King of the Jews

John 18:28-19:16

It is early morning in Jerusalem. In order to avoid ceremonial uncleanness for Passover, the Jews opt not to enter the palace of the Roman governor Herod where Pilate sojourns on his visit to Jerusalem. According to Jewish law, entering a Gentile home or business defiles a man for seven days. This would prevent these leaders from participation in the Passover celebration.[149]

It is interesting to note that the Jews themselves do not have the authority to punish a man by death. Jewish law permits stoning, but this group has not legally condemned Jesus to death. Instead, they are presenting him as a troublemaker to Pilate, someone who is able to stir the crowds in riot against the Roman rule.[150]

They are hoping to secure Pilate's condemnation and a Roman death sentence. A crucifixion places Jesus under the curse of God according to Deuteronomy 21:22-23 and his Messianic claims will be discredited.[151]This is their hope, that at the hands of the Romans, Jesus is eliminated from their midst, they maintain the favor of the people, and their religious standards return to the status quo.

After examining Jesus as to his culpability as a rabble-rouser, Pilate is convinced of his innocence. The Procurator tries to release Jesus four times in John's gospel account, only to be refused each time by the Jewish priests and officials. Even his wife Procula, possibly a convert to Judaism, has dreams of Jesus' innocence and urges Pilate to beware.[152] Eventually, Pilate is threatened outright by the Jews and releases Jesus to the soldiers for crucifixion.

This section highlights the difficult choices that are made during the trial of Jesus. Both Pilate and the Jews must come face to face with their own motivation and the consequential outcomes.

Pontius Pilate

Pilate was a man probably connected with the Roman family of the Pontii, and called "Pilate" from the Latin "pileatus," which was the "cap or badge of a manumitted slave," indicating that he was a "freedman," or the descendant of one. He was the sixth in the order of the Roman procurators of Judea (26-36 A.D.). His headquarters was at Caesarea, but he frequently went up to Jerusalem. Pilate's reign extended over the period of the ministry of John the Baptist and of Jesus Christ.

Pilate hated the Jews whom he ruled, and in times of irritation, freely shed their blood. They responded with mutual hatred and accused him of crime, misadministration, cruelty, and robbery. He visited Jerusalem as seldom as possible for Jerusalem, with its religiousness and ever-smoldering revolt, was a dreary residence for Pilate.

Jesus was brought to the Roman procurator Pilate and he turned Jesus over for crucifixion. By the direction of Pilate an inscription was placed over the cross, stating the crime for which he was crucified, "The King of the Jews."

Afterwards, Pilate's name disappeared from the Gospel history. In 36 A.D. the governor of Syria brought serious accusations against Pilate, and he was banished to Vienne in Gaul, where, according to tradition, he committed suicide.[153]

7. The theme and title of "King" is prevalent in this section of scripture. Examine each group or individual and their opinion and understanding of Jesus as King.

A. Pilate refers to Jesus as king in verses 18:33, 37, 39 and 19:14, 15. How, specifically, does he identify Jesus (verse 33)?

B. The Roman soldiers also call Jesus king in verse 19:1-3. What actions did they take to reinforce their title?

C. The Jewish authorities react to the term king as a designation for Jesus in verses 19:12, and 15. What is their response to Pilate?

D. What does Jesus articulate concerning his kingdom in John 18:36?

8. In defense of their position to crucify Jesus, the Jews tell Pilate that Jesus claims to be *the Son of God* (verse 7). Pilate's Roman mind and mythological beliefs may interpret this statement to mean Jesus is a deity from Olympus. In mythology, Roman deities often consort with mankind and their offspring perform miraculous deeds.[154]

A. What is Pilate's initial reaction (verse 8)?

B. Power and authority become an issue in Pilate's discussion with Jesus. According to Jesus (verse11), who gives Pilate his authority?

C. Who are the ones who have committed a "greater sin" (verse11)?

Scourging

Whipping, scourging, or flogging was a common punishment in Biblical times. First, whipping was a common retribution in the local synagogue. Men and women who committed severe offenses could be beaten as many as 39 times, 26 on the back and 13 on the front. Before the whipping it had to be considered whether the person could stand the punishment. If not, it was reduced to a lesser number. The punishment was administered by the servant of the synagogue, who usually stood on a stone behind the sentenced person. The mode varied, for sometimes the victim would stand by a pillar with his hands tied, sometimes he would bend, sometimes he would be beaten lying down, sometimes he would cower on the seats. The instrument was the lash. Jesus warned his disciples of this type of persecution in Matthew.

The scourging of Jesus is not the synagogue punishment but the Roman "verberatio." The aim of Pilate was to awaken pity by the scourging. It seems as though he wanted to impose only a scourging without crucifixion. According to Roman law the "verberatio" always accompanied a capital sentence along with other degrading punishments and the loss of freedom or civil rights. In many cases it was itself fatal and it usually preceded crucifixion. The number of strokes was not prescribed, but it continued until the flesh hung down in bloody shreds. Slaves administered it, and the condemned person was tied to a pillar. In this case, women were exempted.

The third type of flogging mentioned in the Bible was associated with Paul and the beatings he took in the Book of Acts. These were examinations under torture where he was beaten with a stick.[155]

9. Pilate and the Jews struggle for control over the outcome of Jesus' trial. The Jews are initially evasive as to the exact infringement of their law in John 18:30, but become increasingly hostile as time progresses. The Procurator seeks ways to pacify them, yet is rebuffed in his various attempts.

A. Pilate tries to release Jesus in John 18:31, 39, John 19:6, 12, 14, 15. Conversely, the Jews want him condemned to death by the cross in John 18: 31, 40, John 19:6, 7, 12, and 15. What are some underlying reasons for this resistance (Consider religious, political, financial motivations)?

B. Pilate uses the terminology *I find no basis for a charge against him* in verse 8:38, 19:4 and 6. Find is the word *heureo* meaning to find by enquiry, thought, examination, scrutiny, observation, to find out by practice and experience.[156] *No basis for a charge against him* is simply the word guilt or *aitia* meaning "cause for which one is worthy of punishment, crime."[157] Why is Pilate's viewpoint so different than the Jewish leaders?

10. As Pilate is confronted with the Son of God, he faces a choice, one that challenges his position and his future. The Jews accuse Pilate of being *no friend to Caesar* in John 19:12. This is not just a casual appeal to Pilate's patriotism. To be a "friend to Caesar" denotes a supporter or associate of the emperor, a member of Caesar's inner circle of confidants. If Pilate refuses to act against this usurper Jesus, the Jews will inform Tiberius Caesar, and he, in turn, will question Pilate's loyalty. Tiberius is well known for his suspicious and bitter nature.[158] How are the Jews strong-arming Pilate and what is his response to them?

11. On the feast day, as an act of goodwill, the Roman authorities release one prisoner from a death sentence. The Jews are offered a choice between Jesus and Barabbas. Barabbas is probably a rebel and a resistance fighter against the Roman rule and considered a champion of those who want a free Israel. His name is Aramaic and actually means "son of the father." How would you compare Barabbas' name and nature with Jesus' name as the Son of God in verse 7?

The Crucifixion

John 19:17-42

The growing wave of opposition rooted in the religious hierarchy has reached its zenith. Jesus has been arrested. He has been tried. He has been scourged. He has been sentenced to death by the cross.

The disciples are powerless to stop the injustice that is about to take place. Their expectations of Jesus the Messiah, the one who would establish a new kingdom for Israel, have been shattered. Out of fear and confusion they run.

Pilate turns Jesus over to the execution squad consisting of four legionnaires and a centurion. As he is led through the streets of Jerusalem bearing his cross, Jesus carries a placard that states his name and the nature of his offense. The sign is written in Aramaic, the language of the local populace; it is written in Latin for the officials of Rome; it is written in Greek, the common language or lingua franca of the eastern region. This is eventually fastened to the cross and reads "Jesus of Nazareth, The King of the Jews."[159]

At Golgatha, the place of the skull, Jesus is crucified beside two malefactors. Mark records the time as the third hour or 9 a.m. on Friday morning. Although the precise location of Golgatha is unknown, scripture places it outside of the city, near a major roadway where many pass, and close to a garden where Jesus would be entombed.

During his final moments, Jesus is consciously completing the work the Father has given him. John records the fourth, fifth, and sixth of the Seven Words which Christ speaks from the cross. As the prophecies are fulfilled, Jesus, in complete control, releases his spirit to the Father.

Crucifixion

The beginnings of crucifixion are vague: it seems that the Phoenicians used to tie a criminal to a tree and leave him to die of exposure. The Persians apparently adopted this form of execution from the Phoenicians, the Greeks copied the Persians, and the Romans imitated the Greeks, each adding refinements and making the process more excruciating than the former. In recognition of its degrading nature, Roman law restricted crucifixion to slaves and subjugated people and specifically excluded Roman citizens from this torture and humiliation. This is how Peter could be crucified while Paul had to be beheaded.[160]

The cross consisted of a perpendicular stake with a crossbeam, probably fixed below the top of the stake. In Christ's case there was room for the accusation above His head. A seat or pin was sometimes driven into the stake, or a footrest was affixed to the stake.

The intent of these devices was to delay death for two to three days as a man suspended by his hands suffered loss of blood pressure rapidly and his pulse rate increased. This circumstance was aggravated by the posture, for outstretched arms restricted the lungs' expansion and hampered breathing. If the victim could ease his body by supporting himself on the seat or footrest, he could take a deep breath and circulation was partially restored to the upper body. Exhausted by the effort of raising himself for this breath, he would sag, jerking at the nails through his hands, thus tearing them afresh, aggravating his pain and increasing his torture. The victim's legs were broken when the executioner wanted to hasten death, for this prevented him from supporting his body. Crucifixion was at the same time a means of extreme torture as well as a means of execution; and spectators regarded it as a sport. Spectators reveled in the poor victim's anguished writhing as he died in excruciating pain.[161]

12. The sign proclaiming Jesus' crime stirs a reaction among the Jews. Interpret this new development in light of the battle between Pilate and the Jews over Jesus' sentence of death.

    A. How do the chief priests react and why (verse 21)?

    B. What is Pilate's response?

13. The four legionnaires divide the garments of Jesus among themselves by casting lots. Jesus' wardrobe is composed of five different items: a turban or headdress, an outer robe, a sash or girdle, sandals, and a long tunic woven in one piece that is an undergarment.[162] The soldier's greed contrasts harshly with the pathos of Mary watching her son die a brutal death. Jesus is moved with compassion for his grieving mother as she stands beside her sister Salome, Mary the wife of Clopas, and Mary Magdalene. As the eldest Jewish son, he has carried the responsibility for her well being since Joseph's death. Now, he must entrust her to someone else.

A. Who does Jesus choose to take his place as Mary's son (verse 26-27)?

B. In your opinion, what prompts Jesus in his choice?

14. Jesus' dying words in the Gospel of John complete scriptural prophecy and fulfill his work on earth.

A. He has not had food nor drink since the Passover dinner and his physical strength is failing. In order to fulfill Psalm 69:21, what does Jesus request from the soldiers and what does he receive(verse 29-30)?

B. The Seven Words of Christ on the cross are found in the following scriptures. Record these sayings.

Matthew 27:46

Luke 23:34

Luke 23:43

John 19:26-27

John 19:28

John 19:30

Luke 23:46

15. Romans typically leave criminals on the cross as a warning to those who pass by. However, as a concession to the Jews at this Passover celebration, the soldiers break the legs of the crucified to hasten their death by asphyxiation. Once dead, they are removed from the cross and buried. As they approach Jesus, they realize he is already dead.

A. How does Jesus finally die? Consider John 10:17.

B. Even in death Jesus continues to carry out Old Testament prophecy. According to verse 36 and 37, how are these scriptures fulfilled?

Exodus 12:46

Zechariah 12:10

C. How does Jesus exemplify the Passover lamb (consider Isaiah 53)?

D. How does John distinguish himself as a witness (verse 35) and what is his purpose for testifying?

(John is the one disciple who witnesses the crucifixion. Additional information about the crucifixion is found in the following scripture passages: Matthew 27, Mark 15, Luke 23:26-55)

He is Risen!

John 19:38-20:18

With the Passover celebration at hand and the Sabbath mere hours away, the burial of Jesus has to be expedient. Viewed as a criminal, Jesus will probably be thrown into a common grave with the other two bodies unless someone intervenes.

Throughout the Gospel of John, there is mention of those who are believers in Jerusalem's religious hierarchy. Up to this time they are afraid to openly admit their beliefs, but now two come boldly forward to claim the body of Christ. The first of these two men is Joseph of Arimethea, a town about twenty miles from Jerusalem. According to the other gospel writers, Joseph is a prominent member of the Counsel, rich, a good and upright man who was one who was waiting for the kingdom of God. The other man who comes forward to assist is Nicodemus, who visits Jesus at night (John 3) and defends him before the council (John 7:45-52). He is also a member of the Sanhedrin. These two men bring honor to the lifeless body of Christ while putting themselves at great risk. Because they will touch a dead body, they will not be allowed to participate in the upcoming Passover celebrations.

Three days pass. Chapter 20 opens with Mary Magdalene visiting the garden tomb on that third day, Sunday, the first day of the week on the Jewish calendar. It is common for friends and relatives of the deceased to frequent the gravesite during the first three days. Jewish thought at this time believes that the soul of the departed hovers around the body for three days before departing the earthly tabernacle.[163] What she discovers is, at first, distressing. Then her anguish is turned into joy as she sees her living Savior alive and well.

The miracle of the Resurrection is unique to Christianity. While a few have sacrificed for their faith even to the point of death, no other religion can claim a living Lord. Some try to downplay or rationalize the event by claiming the disciples steal the body, Jesus is not actually dead, or that Jesus' appearance is a vision. However, the evidence is clear that Jesus dies on the cross, is buried in the tomb, and arises on the third day! The impact of Christ's triumph over death, hell, and the grave is the impetus for the remaining disciples to offer their lives in devoted service. All but John will become martyrs for the gospel.

Mary Magdalene

Mary of Magdala, a town on the western shore of the Lake of Tiberias, is noted for the first time in Luke 8:3 as one of the women who "ministered to Christ of their substance." These women accompanied him also on his last journey to Jerusalem and they stood near the cross at the crucifixion. Mary remained till all was over, and the body was taken down and laid in Joseph's tomb.

Again, in the earliest dawn of the first day of the week she came to the sepulcher, bringing with her sweet spices, that she might anoint the body of Jesus. She found the sepulcher empty, but saw the "vision of angels." She lingers thoughtfully, weeping at the door of the tomb when the risen Lord appears to her. His utterance of her name "Mary" recalls her to consciousness, and she utters the joyful, reverent cry, "Rabboni."

This is the last record regarding Mary of Magdala, who now returned to Jerusalem. The idea that this Mary was "the woman who was a sinner," or that she was unchaste, is groundless.[164]

16. It is common for the dead to be laid in a tomb as a form of burial. The limestone rocks and caves that characterize Jerusalem are ideal for this type of interment. How is Jesus prepared for burial (verses 39-40) and where is he laid (verse 41)?

17. Mary Magdalene, or Mary of Magdala, is a follower and faithful disciple of Jesus. Mourning his death, she visits the tomb of Jesus on the first day of the week.

   A. To her amazement, what does she discover?

   B. How does Mary interpret her findings (verse 2)?

   C. Mary remains in the garden to mourn her Lord after returning with Peter and John. She is not just crying or weeping softly, she is wailing (*klaio*) in ritual mourning.[165] As she looks into the tomb, she discovers two angels seated on the limestone tier that holds Jesus' shroud. Why do you think Mary doesn't see Jesus at first?

   D. Jesus has called the eleven men disciples, friends, and now gives them a new designation as his "brothers" in verse 17. How does this terminology reference a new relationship to Christ?

   E. Who is the first post-resurrection evangelist (verse 18)?

18. This portion of scripture records three separate verbs for see. *Blepo*, used in verse 5 and 14, means simply "to be able to see"[166] At first, John merely sees the linen cloths and Mary sees the gardener.

The second word in verse 6 and 12 is *theoreo*, meaning to understand.[167] Peter contemplates or observes the strips of linen, but doesn't know how to interpret them. Mary studies the angels, but hasn't grasped their significance. The third Greek word in verse 8 is *horao*, to perceive.[168]

In verse 8, John _____ and _____.

Final Directives

John 20:19- John 21:25

The post-resurrection visitations of Jesus are recorded in each of the four gospels. Matthew depicts Jesus meeting with the disciples in Galilee. Mark and Luke record Jesus appearing to two unnamed disciples in the country and then to the eleven as they are eating. John documents Jesus materializing twice to his disciples behind closed doors and finally in the early dawn at the Sea of Galilee. The events are memorable and characterize the compassion and concern of the Son of God for his own.

In the Gospel of John, Jesus appears first to his disciples who are hiding behind locked doors. Transcending physical matter with the power of his resurrected body, he greets them with the standard Jewish "Peace be with you" or "Shalom" in Hebrew. Although Jesus' new body is somewhat different in appearance and function, the wounds assure his disciples he is the one who died on the cross. Reaffirming their belief in him, Jesus empowers his disciples as leaders in the Church and equips them for their new apostolic charge.

The disciples return to Galilee. The reasons for this are not certain, but three possibilities exist. First, they may want to escape the watch and hostility of the Jewish authorities in Jerusalem. Second, both Matthew and Mark chronicle Jesus' command to meet him in Galilee, and the disciples act out of obedience. Third, the disciples are discouraged and decide to resume their old occupation of fishing because they have to make a living.[169] Whatever the motivation, the disciples find themselves at the Sea of Galilee awaiting further instructions from Jesus.

The final chapter highlights the restoration of Simon Peter. He is clearly a leader among the disciples, but he is crippled by his past failure. Instead of waiting for Jesus to direct his activities, he presumptuously leads a fishing expedition on the Sea of Tiberius. It ends in failure.

Jesus has already reassured his disciples and reaffirmed their faith, but Peter will require a personal touch. Though he denied his Savior three times, Peter still has a divine purpose in the kingdom of God—his election as apostle remains. But Peter's dismal failure requires healing from the hands of his Master. His rejection of Jesus has branded his soul, and leaves him wanting as the leader he would need to become. Jesus touches the frail and broken humanity of Simon Peter, a man who has stumbled. Restoration comes on the banks of the Sea of Tiberius, once more at a charcoal fire.

Scholars ascertain that Chapter 20 is the original ending to The Gospel of John, and the apostle adds Chapter 21 as an epilogue. The phrase, *If I want him (John) to remain alive until I return, what is that to you?* sparks rumors in the early Church concerning John's longevity. Chapter 21 addresses the issue. In addition, the last chapter completes the restoration of Simon Peter who will spearhead the new evangelistic thrust for the kingdom of God.

19. The disciples are battered in their faith, possibly questioning their commission to preach the gospel. Jesus materializes twice in their midst to confirm and strengthen their wavering faith and equip them to be apostles in the Church.

A. In verse 20:21-23, what three mandates does Jesus give his disciples to prepare them for future ministry?

1.

2.

3.

B. The verb *emphusao*, to breathe on, is the same word used only once in the Old Testament Septuagint (Greek) translation. In Gen 2:7, God breathed on Adam and he became a living soul.[170] How does this empower these apostles who are about to embark on their new mission (verse 22)?

C. Verse 23 is rooted in Rabbinic Judaism. The Rabbis claim the power to pronounce a person either innocent or absolved, or else liable and guilty. They wield this administrative authority in accordance with their position in the Judaic religious structure.[171] In essence, Jesus is transferring this same Rabbinical power in Judaism to his Apostles of the Church. The Son of God extends his earthly authority to those who will bring governmental structure to the infant Church. What purpose will it serve in the future of the Church?

Record these examples of Church authority being exercised.

1 Corinthians 5:4-5

2 Corinthians 2:5-8

1 Timothy 1:20

D. Who needs to physically see and touch Jesus in order to believe (20:25)?

Simon Peter

Peter was a Galilean fisherman, the son of John and brother of Andrew. The brothers came from the village of Bethsaida. They had been disciples of John the Baptist before they became disciples of Jesus. Peter was married and owned a house in Capernaum.[172]

The Galileans had a reputation for independence and energy. They were frank, blunt, more transparent, impetuous, and simple. Simon was a genuine Galilean. He spoke the peculiar dialect, reckoned harsh in Judea. The Galilean accent stuck to Simon all through his career. It betrayed him as a follower of Christ when he stood within the judgment-hall and it betrayed his own nationality on the day of Pentecost.[173]

Peter took the lead in the new Christian community. He was the principal preacher as demonstrated at Pentecost, the spokesman before the Jewish authorities, and the president in the administration of discipline.

Though the church as a whole made a deep impression on the community, it was to Peter in particular that supernatural powers were attributed. As a response to a vision from God, Peter visits the house of Cornelius and was the first apostle to be associated with Gentile evangelism.[174] Tradition holds that Peter died as a martyr in Rome, probably under Nero in 64 A.D.

20. Simon Peter decides to go out to fish and the others answer, "We'll go with you." After toiling all night with the nets, they catch nothing. Yet, at the direction of Jesus, they secure 153 fish with just one cast of their nets.

A. Simon Peter leads the others to fish, yet their efforts are fruitless. How does Simon's current wounded state possibly effect his leadership?

B. As Jesus interacts with his disciples from shore, John, *the disciple whom Jesus loves*, perceives that the man is the Lord. What title of address does Jesus use to call to his disciples (verse 5)? How is this noteworthy?

C. How does Simon Peter react when he learns it is Jesus on shore?

21. Simon Peter splashes to the shore, eager to see his Lord and Master. What awaits him (a charcoal fire in the early morning) may be a startling reminder of the haunting incident of Passover morning. For healing to occur, Jesus must return Peter to the time and place of his mishap.

A. How is the scene on the shore similar to the picture of Peter's denial?

B. The disciples knew of Peter's denial, therefore, the renewal Jesus performs in their presence reassures them of Peter's position among them. With each successive question of Simon's love, Jesus probes deeper into the heart of his servant. How many times does Jesus ask Peter if he loved him? Why is this significant?

C. Jesus addresses Simon Peter not as Simon the "Rock," but as Simon son of John. By disregarding his own nickname for Simon, Jesus speaks to the man, not to Simon Peter the Apostle. How is this relevant to the healing process?

D. The third question brings an emotional response from Simon as Jesus pierces his festering wound. The word hurt in verse 17 is *lupeo* meaning pain and sorrow. Both physical pain and mental anguish are covered by the word.[175]How has Jesus exposed this hidden injury? What is Simon's response?

E. Intertwined with the healing process is the commissioning of Simon Peter. In the first and third question (verses 15 and 17), Jesus directs Peter to "feed" the lambs and the sheep. *Bosko* stands for feed, portraying the duty of a Christian teacher to promote in every way the spiritual welfare of the members of the church.[176] The second question of love elicits a different command. This word is *poimaino*, to feed, to tend a flock, to rule, govern, to serve the body.[177] Describe the responsibilities Jesus is giving to Peter.

22. As a conclusion to Simon Peter's healing and commission, Jesus' final directive to Peter stirs some questions in Peter's mind.

A. Why does Peter ask concerning John (verses 20-21)?

B. What are Jesus final commanding words to Peter?

C. How are these words vital to Peter's Christian walk, as well as our own?

119

Love

"Agape" is the principal Greek word used for love in the New Testament. Of the three words for love in the Hellenistic world, it was the least common. The other two words were "eros," which meant sexual love, and "philos," which meant friendship and personal affection, although their meanings could vary according to the context in which they appeared.

Agape, because it was used so seldom and was so unspecific in meaning, was often used in the New Testament to designate the unmerited, univeral love God shows to humankind in sending his son as suffering redeemer. When used of human love, it means selfless and self-giving love.[178]

When Jesus says, "Do you love me?" in his first and second question, he uses the Greek word agapas. When Simon answers, he uses the Greek word philo (I love). In Jesus' third and final question to Peter, he ,too, uses the word philo.

The distinction between these two Greek words is described as follows: Agapas reflects more of judgment and deliberate choice; philo has more of attachment and peculiar personal affection. The "Do you love me?" (agapas) on the lips of the Lord seems to Peter at this moment too cold a word, as though his Lord were keeping him at a distance, or at least not inviting him to draw near, as in the passionate yearning of his heart he desired now to do. Therefore, he substitutes his own stronger "I love" (philo) in its place. A second time he does the same. When the Lord demands a third time whether he loves him, he does it in the word that will satisfy Peter ("Do you love me?" phileo). It alone claims from Jesus that personal attachment and affection that Peter seeks.[179]

Making it Personal

Expectations. We all have them in one form or another—expectations of people, members of our family, those who are friends, and fellow workers—expectations of ourselves expressed as visions, dreams, goals—and even expectations of our God.

When I was a young girl, I loved to fish with my father. I can fondly remember baiting a hook and sitting beneath a shaded grove patiently waiting for that first bite. As a result, when my family and I go on vacation, we try to include a fishing expedition in the agenda. I always expect to catch my limit!

One particular camping trip to a Georgia mountain lake, I had prayed and asked God to bless our time together, and especially to bless the fishing. For three days, we stood on the campground pier with baited hooks, but caught nothing. I was so discouraged. My husband suggested we try the streams in the surrounding area for trout, but I was determined to catch the "big" fish on the lake. On the last night of our trip, we sat at a restaurant and overheard a conversation about the phenomenal fishing two families had discovered while angling in the nearby streams. Apparently, the local hatchery was seeding the streams with fish, but their truck had the misfortune to break down. All of the fish that should have been transported across the state had to be emptied locally in the brooks. God had answered my prayer, but I was unable to "see" the answer because my expectations had been elsewhere.

Where are your expectations? Have you occasionally missed the Lord because the package wasn't wrapped the way you imagined? It didn't come through the channel you anticipated? Or maybe it seemed so insignificant that it was overlooked. Just like the disciples, we must rid ourselves of preconceived formulas of God and allow him to work freely in our best interest.

23. Identify one of your expectations that came in an unpredicted way.

    A. In what way was it surprising?

    B. How did this change your concept of God's grace in your life?

    C. What are you hopefully anticipating now?

    D. Do you have any preconceived ideas that need to be discarded?

24. Choices direct our lives. Our motivation, the decisions themselves, and the resulting consequences weave a lifelong tapestry. We are the product today of our decisions we made yesterday. Pilate was faced with a difficult choice—make the "right" decision and let an innocent man go free or protect himself and his political position. In this case, the "right" decision required sacrifice on the part of Pilate, something he was not willing to do.

    A. Have you ever been faced with this type of decision? What did you decide?

    B. What was the outcome?

    C. Reflect on what you gained in return for your sacrificial stance.

25. Peter suffered with a wound that was not visible. It lay beneath the surface of his exterior, festering away at his confidence and relationship to God, the source of vitality for his life. Although it could not be readily seen on the surface, Peter's wound impaired his vision, influenced his direction, and weakened his leadership effectiveness.

What prevents you from succeeding in life? What keeps you tethered to a stake in the ground instead of having the freedom to soar as an eagle? Is it a deplorable action or perhaps an even more regrettable inaction? Is it words spoken in anger under emotional distress or even statements others have made about you? What comes to mind as an obstacle to your growth and spiritual health as a Christian?

The gospel of good news still includes the healing power of Jesus. He is the same yesterday, today, and forever. What Jesus did for Peter on the shores of Tiberius, he can do for you today as you yield yourself to his ministrations. Find a quiet place where you can commune with God. Use the following directives as a guideline for prayer:

1. What is the source of your physical or emotional pain? This may be a specific incident, certain words, etc.

2. Forgive those who are involved. Jesus commands us to forgive, but do not confuse forgiveness with acceptance. God is not telling you to believe what occurred was proper or tolerable. He is asking you to release it into his hands. The word "forgive" actually means, "to release." By forgiving, you disentangle yourself from the problem so that you may be healed.

3. Ask the Lord to touch the very root of your pain and suffering with his healing touch. (Allow God to minister to you personally and completely).

4. Pray and release the offenders into God's hands once again. Ask God to sever any unhealthy ties that still bind you to the incident.

5. Ask the Lord to restore your emotions and your physical health. Be specific in your request and wait on his presence.

6. Ask God if there is anything he wants you to do to help facilitate your healing-make a phone call, write a letter, pray for those who have hurt you, etc.

7.Thank God for his wonderful healing touch and spend a few moments praising and worshipping him.

26. Take a moment to record your reflections on the trial and crucifixion. Consider the immensity of Jesus' sacrifice, the injustice, the pain, and isolation.

Jesus,

I cannot imagine the suffering, the pain, and the shame that you bore for me on the cross. I am overwhelmed that your love for mankind, and especially for me, was the strength that prepared you to lay down your life in this way. Because you died bearing my sin, I no longer have to carry that sin nature within me. And because you rose again from the grave, I can live anew in you.

You were pierced for my transgressions; you were crushed for my iniquities. The chastisement that brings me peace was upon you, and by your stripes I am healed.

Thank you, Lord, for bearing what I will never have to bear and suffering in ways I will never have to suffer. Help me to be strong in my stance for righteousness. When I have the opportunity to declare your grace and power, may I have the courage to boldly proclaim that you are the Son of God. Glorify yourself in and through me.

Amen

Notes

_____

_____

_____

_____

_____

_____

_____

_____

_____

_____

Closing Comments

*A*t the close of this study, you may ask yourself, "What does Jesus want from my life?" "What is my place in his kingdom?" "How and where do I follow?"

First, Jesus wants you whole and well, able to enjoy your life, the life he gives abundantly. You may need to visit your own "charcoal fire" and allow Jesus to lance the festering boil in your heart and soul.

Second, you do have a vibrant, fruitful place in his kingdom designed especially for you, your talents and gifts. Start where you are. Embrace what he has placed in your hand to do today. Be faithful to that calling and you will grow into greater things.

Third, be patient. The promises of God come by faith and patience. Be obedient to the call and direction of God as it arises. The well-seasoned fruit of a mature Christian takes time to grow. God is not as interested in what you do as he is in what you are.

Fourth, enjoy the process. Each step has its own blessings and challenges. You will never arrive at that final destination so enjoy each stop along the way.

Fifth, be blessed and realize there is a God who loves you. In spite of all your imperfections, your successes and failures, God's love is constant, perfect and unwavering. Rest in his love and allow his presence to be a constant companion throughout your life.

Closing Prayer:

Thank you, Father, for your great love expressed though your son Jesus. He was your gift to the world. I recognize Jesus as my Savior and welcome his presence into my life.

Thank you, Lord Jesus for being my example in godly living. You show me your ways and encourage me to walk as you did so many years ago. Help me to continue to grow and know you in a deeper way. Your truth sets me free.

Thank you, Holy Spirit, for your constant presence in my life. Teach me. Reveal yourself to me. Help me to hear your voice and follow you.

I choose to live my life in the light of your word. I choose life which you gave so freely thousands of years ago and yet still continue to offer today. I choose the kingdom of light, the glorious kingdom of God and all of its power and glory which you purchased for me on the cross.

I reverently bow before you. I give you my gratitude for all that you have done in my life and all that you will continue to do. You are good and your goodness will be with me always.

Amen

Endnotes

Chapter One

1 Johannes P. Louw and Eugene A. Nida, *Greek-English Lexicon of the New Testament Based on Semantic Domains, electronic ed.* (New York: United Bible Societies, 1988).
2 Paul Enns, *The Moody Handbook of Theology, electronic ed.* (Chicago: Moody Press, 1996).
3 *The New Bible Dictionary, electronic ed.* (Wheaton: Tyndale House Publishers, Inc., 1962).
4 Frank E. Gaebelein, *The Expositor's Bible Commentary: Vol. 9* (Grand Rapids: Zondervan Publishing House, 1981), 5.

Chapter Two

5 Gaebelein, 29.
6 William A. Simmons, *New Testament Survey* (Cleveland: Lee College, 1994), 102.
7 Enns, 415-16.
8 Louw & Nida, LN 37.19. 10.
9 G. Kittel, G. W. Bromiley & G. Friedrich, Ed., *Theological Dictionary of the New Testament: Vol. 4* (Grand Rapids: Eerdmans),10.
10 C. F. Pfeiffer & E. F. Harrison, *The Wycliffe Bible Commentary : New Testament* (Chicago: Moody Press, 1962), Jn 1:12.
11 Kittel, Bromiley & Friedrich, Vol. 1, 689.
12 Strong, electronic ed.
13 Ibid.
14 Strong, electronic edition
15 Wood & Marshall, 433.
16 R. Jamieson, A. R. Fausset & D. Brown, A Commentary, *Critical and Explanatory, on the Old and New Testaments* (Oak Harbor: Logos Research Systems, Inc., 1997), John 1:14.

Chapter Three

17 Strong, electronic ed.
18 Achtemeier, 827.
19 Gaebelein, 36.
20 *The New Bible Dictionary, electronic ed.*
21 Achtemeier, 501-02.
22 Wood & Marshall, 277-78.
23 Easton, electronic ed.
24 Gaebelein, 41.
25 Wood & Marshall, 996.

Chapter Four

26 Edersheim, 254-57.
27 Strong, electronic ed.
28 Easton, electronic ed.
29 W. W. Wiersbe, *The Bible Exposition Commentary, electronic edition.* (Wheaton: Victor Books, 1989)
30 Gabelein, 47
31 Wiersbe, electronic ed.
32 Strong, electronic ed.
33 Enhanced Strong's Lexicon, electronic ed.
34 Ibid.
35 Enhanced Strong's Lexicon, electronic ed.
36 R.L. Thomas, *New American Standard Hebrew-Aramaic and Greek Dictionaries: Updated Edition, electronic ed.* (Anaheim: Foundation Publications, Inc., 1998).
37 Ralph Gower, *The New Manners and Customs of Bible Times: Student Edition* (Chicago: Moody Press, 2000). 202-03
38 Gaebelein, 56.
39 Edersheim, 216-19.
39 Gower, 202-03.
40 Strong, electronic ed.

Chapter Five

41 Edersheim, 244-45.
42 Gaebelein, 42.
43 Strong, electronic ed.
44 William C. Martin, *The Layman's Bible Encyclopedia* (Nashville: The Southwestern Company, 1964), 121.
45 Gaebelein, 60.
46 Easton, electronic ed.
47 Edersheim, 321.
48 Alfred Edersheim, *The Temple: Its Ministries and Services* (Peabody: Hendrickson Publishers, Inc., 1994), 1046-56. From this point forward all references to this particular work of Edersheim will be distinguished with its title. Any other references correspond to The Life and Times of Jesus the Messiah.
49 Gaebelein, 67.
50. Kittel, Bromiley & Friedrich, Vol. 1, 219.
51 Wood & Marshall, 434-35.
52 Louw& Nida, electronic ed.
53 W. Arndt, F. W. Gingrich, F. W. Danker & W. Bauer, *A Greek-English Lexicon of the New Testament and Other Early Christian Literature* (Chicago:University of Chicago Press, 1979), 870.

54 Mills, electronic ed.
55 Gower & Wright, electronic ed.
56 Edersheim, 598.
57 Gower & Wright, electronic ed.
58 Edersheim, 601-02.
59 Edersheim, 692.
60 Gaebelein, 118.
61 Edersheim, 693-96.
62 Edersheim, 696-97.
63 Edersheim, 856-58

Chapter Six

64 L. Richards and L.O. Richards, *The Teacher's Commentary, electronic ed.* (Wheaton: Victor Books, 1987).
65 Edersheim, 494.
66 Brooke Foss Westcott, *The Gospel According to St. John, The Greek Text with Introduction and Notes, Vol. 1,* (Grand Rapids: William B. Eerdmans Publishing Company, 1954), 226.
67 Gaebelein, 77.
68 Edersheim, 495.
69 Gower & Wright, electronic ed.
70 Easton, electronic ed.
71 Edersheim, 495.
72 Enns, electronic ed.
73 Strong, electronic ed.
74 Edersheim, *The Temple: Its Ministry and Services*, 25.
75 Arrington & Stronstad, 52.
76 Edersheim, 588-89.
77 Achtmeier, 546.
78 Edersheim, 224.
79 Kittel, Friedrich & Bromiley, 225.
80 Louw & Nida, LN 37.135.
81 Wood & Marshall, 8.
82 Gower & Wright, electronic ed.
83 Strong, electronic ed.
84 Richards & Richards, Jn 13:1.
85 Achtemeier, 937-38.
86 Strong, electronic ed.
87 Kittel, Bromiley & Friedrich, Volume 3, 754.
88 Strong, electronic ed.
89 Kittel, Bromiley & Friedrich, 533.
90 Ibid., 532.
91 Strong, electronic edition.
92 Ibid.
93 Strong, electronic edition.
94 Ibid.
95 Strong, electronic edition.
96 Gaebelein, 109.
97 Achtmeier, 216.
98 Strong, electronic ed.
99 Ibid.
100 Easton, electronic ed.
101 Swanson, electronic ed.
102 Strong, electronic ed.
103 Ibid.
104 Swanson, electonic edition.
105 Gaebelein, 150.
106 Ibid,154.
107 Achtemeier, 1112-1113.
108 Swanson, electronic ed.
109 Gaebelein, 151.
110 Strong, electronic ed.
111 Ibid.
112 Strong, electronic edition.
113 Wood & Marshall, 902.

Chapter Seven

114 M. Mills, *The Life of Christ : A Study Guide to the Gospel Record, electronic ed.* (Dallas: 3E Ministries, 1999).
115 Achtemeier, 719.
116 Mills, electronic edition.
117 Swanson, electronic ed.
118. Ibid
119 Edersheim, 815-22.
120 Mills, electronic edition.
121 Kittel, Bromiley & Friedrich,Volume 4, 594.
122 Strong, electronic ed.

123 Easton, electronic ed.
124 Strong, electronic edition.
125 Ibid
126 Achtemeier, 401.
127 Strong, electronic ed.
128 Swanson, electronic edition.
129 Easton, electronic ed.
130 Wood & Marshall, 899.
131 Gaebelein,161.
132 Easton, electronic ed.
133 Wood & Marshall, 949.
134 Strong, electronic ed.
135 Swanson, electronic ed.
136 Ibid.
137 Swanson, electronic ed.
138 Ibid.
139 Gaebelein, 164.
140 Strong, electronic ed.
141 Gabelein, 166.
142 Merriam-Webster, *Merriam Webster's Collegiate Dictionary, electronic ed.* (Springfield: Merriam Webster, 1933).

Chapter Eight

143 Gaebelein, 168.
144 Edersheim, 847-48.
145 Edersheim, 851-52.
146 Strong, electronic ed.
147 Edersheim, 858.
148 Gaebelein, 171.
149 Gaebelein, 174.
150 Edersheim, 858-59.
151 Gaebelein, 175.
152 Edersheim, 867.
153 Easton, electronic ed.
154 Gaebelein, 177.
155 Kittel, Bromiley & Friedrich, Volume 4, 517.
156 Strong, electronic ed.
157 Ibid.
158 Gaebelein, 178.
159 Ibid, 180-81.
160 Mills, electronic ed.
161 Ibid.
162 Gaebelein, 181
163 Edersheim, 907.
164 Easton, electronic ed.
165 Swanson, electronic ed.
166 Ibid
167 Swanson, electronic ed.
168 Ibid.
169 Gaebelein, 199.
170 Strong, electronic ed.
171 Edersheim, 917.
172 Achtemeier, 776.
173 Easton, electronic ed.
174 Wood & Marshall, 907.
175 Kittel, Bromiley & Friedrich, 540.
176 Strong, electronic ed.
177 Ibid.
178 Achtemeier, 14.
179 Easton, electronic ed.

Bibliography

Achtmeier, P. J. *Harper's Bible Dictionary.* San Francisco: Harper & Row Publishers, 1985.

Arndt, W., Gingrich, F. W., Danker, F. W. and Bauer, W. *A Greek-English Lexicon of the New Testament and Other Early Christian Literature.* Chicago: University of Chicago Press, 1979.

Arrington, French L. & Stronstad, Roger. *Full Life Bible Commentary to the New Testament.* Grand Rapids: Zondervan Publishing House, 1999.

Beers, V. Gilbert. *The Book of Life: Return to the Land, Volume 15.* Grand Rapids: The Zondervan Corporation, 1980.

Connolly, Peter. *Living in the Times of Jesus of Nazareth.* Israel: Steinmatzky Ltd., 1983.

Easton, M. *Easton's Bible Dictionary, electronic ed.* Oak Harbor: Logos Research Systems , Inc., 1996.

Edersheim, Alfred, *The Life and Times of Jesus the Messiah.* Peabody: Hendrickson Publishers, Inc.,1997.

Enhanced Strong's Lexicon. Oak Harbor: Logos Research Systems, Inc., 1995.

Enns, Paul. *The Moody Handbook of Theology*, electronic ed. Chicago: Moody Press, 1996.

Gaebelein, Frank E. *The Expositor's Bible Commentary: Volume 9.* Grand Rapids: Zondervan Publishing House, 1981.

Gower, Ralph. *The New Manners and Customs of Bible Times: Student Edition.* Chicago: Moody Press, 2000.

Jamieson, R., Fausset, A. R. & Brown, D. *A Commentary, Critical and Explanatory, on the Old and New Testaments.* Oak Harbor: Logos Research Systems, Inc., 1997.

Kittel, G., Bromiley, G. W. & Friedrich, G. Ed., *Theological Dictionary of the New Testament: Volume 1-10.* Grand Rapids: William B. Eerdmans Publishing Company, 1964.

Kittel, G. and Friedrich, G. *The Theological Dictionary of the New Testament, Abridged in One Volume, electronic ed.* Grand Rapids: William B. Eerdmans Publishing Company, 1985.

Louw, Johannes P. & Nida, Eugene A. *Greek-English Lexicon of the New Testament Based on Semantic Domains, electronic ed.* New York: United Bible Societies, 1988.

Martin, William C. *The Layman's Bible Encyclopedia.* Nashville: The Southwestern Company, 1964.

Mills, M. *The Life of Christ: A Study Guide to the Gospel Record, electronic ed.* Dallas: 3E Ministries,1999.

The New Bible Dictionary, electronic ed. Wheaton: Tyndale House Publishers, Inc., 1962.

Pfeiffer, C. F. & Harrison, E.F. *The Wycliffe Bible Commentary: New Testament.* Chicago: Moody Press,1962.

Richards, L. & Richards, L. O. *The Teacher's Commentary, electronic ed.* Wheaton: Victor Books, 1987.

Simmons, William A. *New Testament Survey*, Cleveland: Lee University, 1994.

Strong, J. *The Exhaustive Concordance of the Bible, electronic ed.* Ontario: Woodside Bible Fellowship,1996.

Swanson, J. *Dictionary of Biblical Languages With Semantic Domains, electronic ed.* Oak Harbor: Logos Research Systems, Inc., 1997.

Tan, P. I. *Encyclopedia of 7700 Illustrations: A Treasury of Illustrations, Anecdotes, Facts and Quotations for Pastors, Teachers, and Christian Workers, electronic ed.* Garland: Bible Communications, 1979.

Thomas, R. L. *New American Standard Hebrew-Aramaic and Greek Dictionaries: Updated Edition,electronic ed.* Ananheim: Foundation Publications, Inc., 1998.

Westcott, Brooke Foss. *The Gospel According to John, The Greek Text with Introduction and Notes, Volume One.* Grand Rapids: William B. Eerdmans Publishing Company, 1954.

Wiersbe, W. W. *The Bible Exposition Commentary, electronic ed.* Wheaton: Victor Books, 1989.

Wood, D. R. & Marshall, I. H. *New Bible Dictionary, electronic ed.* Downer's Grove: Inter Varsity Press,

1996.

About the Author

What happens when Joyce Meyer meets Beth Moore? Meet Pam Palagyi! She is practical, personal, and believes the word of God is the standard for daily living.

As a speaker and author, Pam has been inspiring audiences nationally and abroad since 1998. Through leadership, personal growth seminars, mentoring, and conferences, she has equipped and encouraged others to excel in their personal fields of interest.

Pam has a diverse background in training and leadership development. She has experience as a pastor, has created and administrated three Christian training centers, and mentored interns from around the world. Pam is gifted in organizational development and team formation. Her international experience spans five continents where she trained, encouraged, and imparted biblical principles to other pastors and leaders. She has also led mission teams for evangelism and church planting.

Pam earned a Master of Divinity degree from Regent University. She is trained in personality assessment, and is a graduate of CLASS (Christian Leaders, Authors, and Speaker Seminar) seminar programs. Pam holds a lifelong certification from Evangelical Training Association and a Certificate of Achievement as a Senior Pastor from Church Leader Insights Coaching Network. Pam is also a certified instructor of the Streams 101 course, The Art of Hearing God.

Her published works include *Established: Seeking God's Plan for Spiritual Growth, Empowered: Igniting the Fire for Practical Ministry, The Word Became Flesh: A Study of the Gospel of John, 7 Easy Steps to Goal Setting Success,* and *Tucker, The Amazing Dog.*

Pam is also a contributor to the devotional *Life in the Spirit,* Charles Stanley's *In Touch* magazine, CBN online magazine, *The Southbridge Evening News,* and a columnist for *The Sturbridge Times.* She studies writing and the publication process and has become a mentor for other aspiring writers.,

Pam is blessed with a wonderful family, two daughters and two granddaughters who she loves to spoil! With her husband Paul, she enjoys working around the home, creative hobbies, golfing, biking, travel, and a good movie...with lots of popcorn!

Pam Palagyi YouTube

Pam Palagyi .com

The Aspiring Writer
Equipping and Encouraging the Writer in You
www.theaspiringwriter.com

The Leadership Ladder
Moving Forward, Stepping Up
www.theleadershipladder.com

Other Books by Pam Palagyi

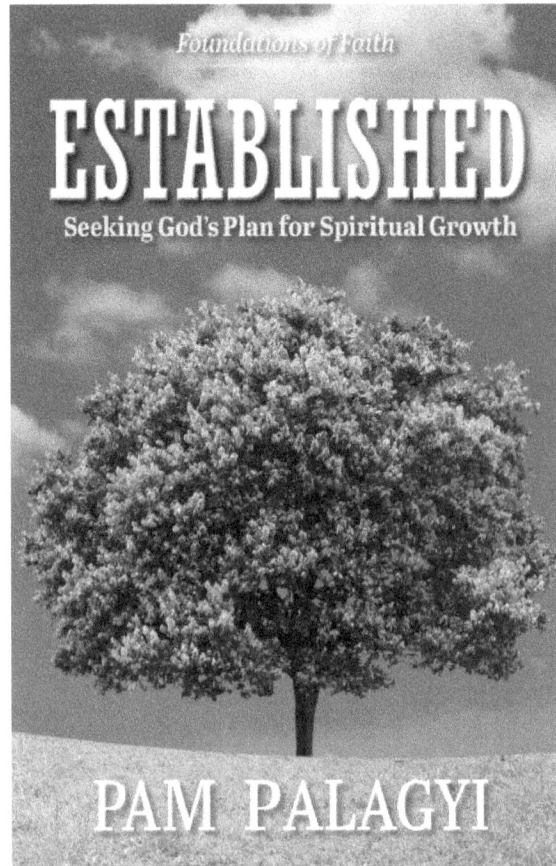

Are you experiencing all that God has to offer?

Have you asked yourself questions like...

> *Who am I and how do I relate to God?*

> *Do I have a destiny, a God-directed plan for my life?*

> *How can I overcome the daily obstacles and difficulties?*

God created a perfect world. He planned for us to live a dynamic and fulfilled life within that realm. If your present lifestyle falls short of his best, then it is time to revisit the original design!

Established: Seeking God's Plan for Spiritual Growth unveils God's blueprint for success. When life began in the Garden of Eden, God provided five key elements essential to his plan. And you have a personal invitation to rediscover this garden!

Bonus...*30 Day Devotional Guide*

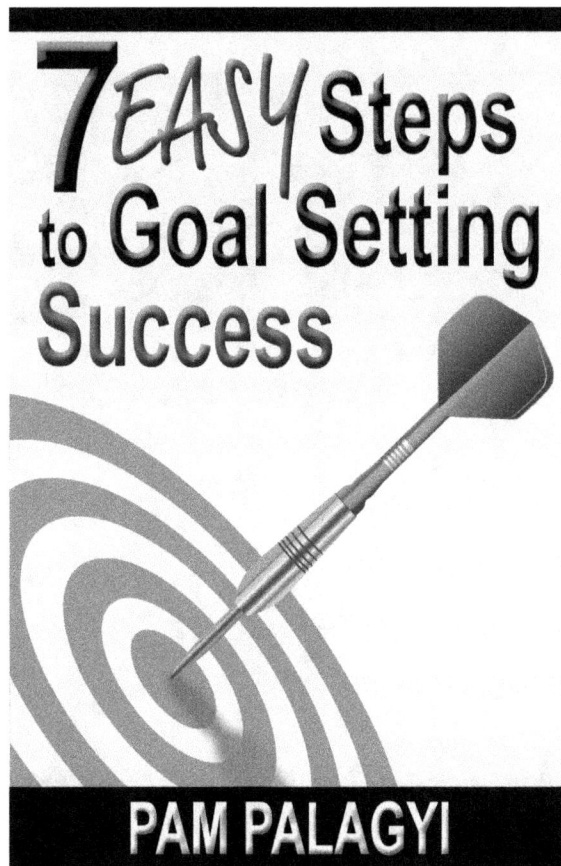

7 EASY Steps to Goal Setting Success
PAM PALAGYI

7 Easy Steps to Goal Setting Success will help you choose your targets, implement specific actions, and follow through to achieve those goals. 7 Easy Steps is a process that helps draw a road map for your future. After you have completed all 7 steps, you will have in your hands...

A life outline of your hopes, dreams, and desires on customized forms.

An overview of your goals for the next 365 days.

A 90 Day Action Plan to propel you forward.

In this comprehensive guide to setting goals, you will discover...

10 reasons why people set goals.

How to choose the B.E.S.T. goals.

6 Life Systems that influence your success.

A healthy and balanced approach to living.

"For I know the plans I have for you," declares the LORD, "plans to prosper you and not to harm you, plans to give you hope and a future." Jeremiah 29:11

When we can tap into God's plan for our life, all things become possible!

Bonus...*Goal Setting Workbook*

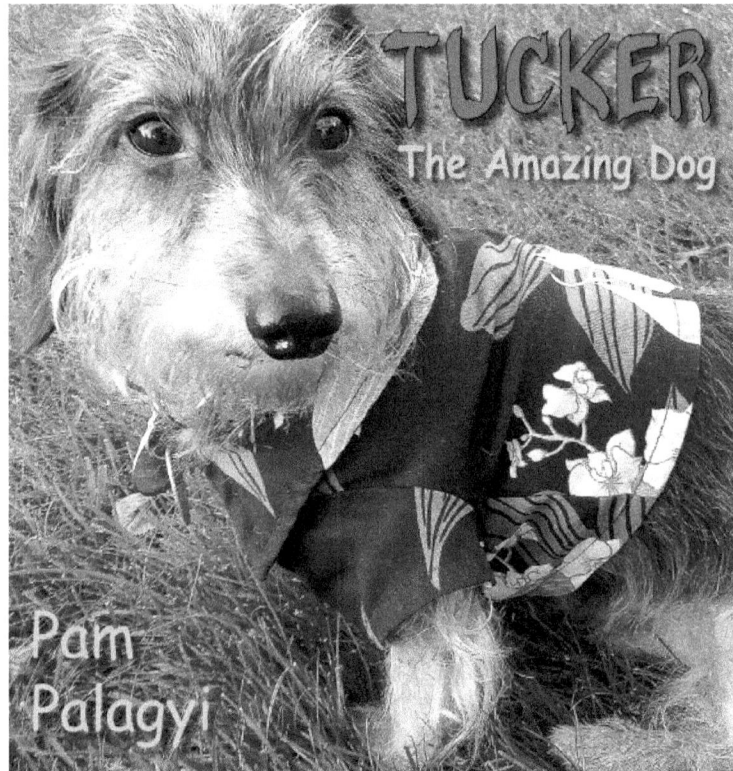

TUCKER
The Amazing Dog

Pam Palagyi

Meet Tucker...

the long-haired, wire-haired, little dachshund with a BIG personality! Join in the fun as Tucker eats, sleeps, and does tricks in his own delightful way!

www.ingramcontent.com/pod-product-compliance
Lightning Source LLC
LaVergne TN
LVHW081333060426
835513LV00014B/1273